MW00947153

STANDING IN THE WAY

From Trafficking Victim to Human Rights Activist

BY ANJALI TAMANG AND SARAH SYMONS

Dedicated to Smita Singh: defender, sister and friend

Copyright 2020 - Wallsend Publishing

What stands in the way becomes the way

Marcus Aurelius

Out of suffering have emerged the strongest souls;
the most massive characters are seared with scars

Kahlil Gibran

Introduction

When I was eleven years old, I was trafficked from a village in Nepal to a brothel in Kolkata, India. For two years, I endured nightly rapes, beatings, hunger and psychological manipulation. Abandoning all hope was the only way to survive.

There are no words to describe the pain of that time. The scars of that experience will always be with me, written on my soul, and on my body.

I don't remember the details of every night, every customer who thoughtlessly laughed as he stole away another piece of me, leaving me a little more bruised, a little less whole. My memories of that time are shrouded in a dark fog...physical pain, a deep longing for home and family, dashed hopes like a weight on my chest, the actual weight of men's bodies on my small frame, constant fear, lies and betrayal. And always, always a deep feeling of shame.

My name is Anjali Tamang, and I am twenty-five years old. To look at me today, you would not see that wounded child, crying soundlessly on a stained mattress, wrapped in a thin sheet. You would not see a victim, or even a survivor fighting her way to wellness. You would see a teacher and college student, a young mother and wife, a sister and friend, a woman of faith, an advocate for the poor and vulnerable. I hope you would see a person who stands for love.

My journey from that dark and hopeless place to the meaningful and joyful life that I live today is an absolute miracle. Every day that I wake up *not* in that brothel is a beautiful and miraculous day. The life I lead today is a precious gift because usually, girls from my community who are trafficked to India never come back.

Even if girls do eventually return home, the horror of the experience has swallowed their identity and spirit. They are like *pisaj* - a ghost from Nepali folklore - who must consume others in order to survive. The trafficked become the traffickers, feeding on the next generation. Selling girls has become so normal in our district, that the great majority of girls end up either trafficked to India or forced into child marriages to prevent them from being trafficked.

My birthplace is in the Eastern side of the country, in the foothills of the Himalayas. I am glad that I was born in such a beautiful place. My village is graced with bright white snow and deep green forests, but far away from the light of education. Due to illiteracy, and a breakdown of social values, people cannot separate what is right and what is wrong for their lives. They want to spend their whole lives enjoying themselves and making money. They are willing to sell their daughters and sisters in order to be rich or to compete with others in wealth and build a house.

In my area, the main ethnic group are the Tamang. Agriculture is the main occupation. People don't need to buy much from the market or from the city, because they have land where they can grow anything. They rear

3

goats, sheep, oxen, cattle and buffalo. Almost everyone works in the fields from morning to night. Children go to the forest to harvest grass in the cold mornings instead of going to school.

Subsistence farming has been the livelihood of the Tamang for centuries, as long as anyone can remember. However, for the past few decades, a different, and destructive livelihood has been growing: the selling of girls for forced prostitution.

First, girls are made to leave their homes. Families force or coerce girls to marry around the age of ten. The men who marry these small girls are much older. Parents often ask the husbands not to force sexual relations on their daughters. The man, or his family, will answer, "In that case, we cannot take your daughter in marriage, but you can always send her to a brothel in India". This is something that people take far too lightly.

Child marriage is a gateway to trafficking for many girls. Others are tricked by traffickers, or sold by neighbors, or by their own relatives. Some go willingly, thinking that they will be doing another kind of work, like housekeeping or working in a restaurant. They think they will be able to send money home to help their families.
When young girls are taken from their home, village and family, they have no one to protect them, so they are easy prey for traffickers. Coming from remote villages with little contact with the larger world, they don't have the knowledge or experience to run away, or to resist.

Tamang girls are fiercely loyal to their families. If they believe their parents have sent them to work in brothels, then that is what they will do. They won't even try to escape.

People from my village truly do not understand what it means for a young girl to work in a brothel, or what she will endure there. They can't imagine the brutality of the pimps and madams, or the careless violence of the customers. Some girls get pregnant in the brothels. Many die from sexually transmitted diseases, or other diseases like tuberculosis.

The first few years in a brothel, girls are locked inside, and forced to service many customers. They have no control over their lives. They earn little or no money. They are beaten, deprived of sleep, and kept hungry to keep them weak and terrified. They are given alcohol or drugs to keep them numb and compliant. In time, drugs and alcohol become a habit. Some girls come to believe that they are worthless, so they drink themselves to death.

Eventually, to avoid the pain or to get a respite from the abuse, the girls become traffickers themselves. They return to their villages, talking about the glamorous life they enjoyed in India. They help to trick families, and they buy new girls for the brothels. How can they so quickly forget their pain? How could they do the terrible things to other girls that people did to them?

Part of the problem is that women who have been exploited cannot find other jobs in the villages. They have no education, skills or training to do any other kind of work. They feel they have no other choice but to victimize other girls in order to help their own families. Hurting people hurt others.

My path is very different, by the grace of God, and because of the love and courage of many wonderful people. Their stories are woven together with mine, in this book and in real life.

The fact that I was trafficked was no random event. There were many things that made me vulnerable. The lack of education and awareness in my community was a major factor. Today, as I share my story with the world, I am also returning to my village to open a school, so that the next generation of girls can get an education, rather than being sent to India to earn money in the most brutal and dehumanizing way.

The things that stood in my way - trafficking and violence, the loss of my childhood and many other bitter losses - have *become my way forward*. The suffering I endured, and the healing I received, have given me the strength and the experience to take action against child trafficking.

I will fight to my last breath to protect the next generation of children in my community. I share my story now to help prevent this from happening to other children, anywhere in the world.

Chapter 1

When I close my eyes, I can't recall my father's face, but I can see his legs. I remember sitting on his lap as he read to me. Those were such happy times for me.

In my family were my parents, my brother who is two years older, and me. My name is Anjali, but back then everyone called me Mendo, which means flower. I was small for my age, and very thin. I had the straight black hair, wide-set eyes and fair skin which are typical of Nepal's mountain people.

My mother told us that her childhood had been very difficult. She was the eldest of eight children, and her family was desperately poor. They had to travel a whole day just to buy salt. Although she used to work hard in the fields day and night, her family never had enough food, and she was always hungry. Maybe that constant hunger broke something in my mother. She was never able to love me the way that I wanted and needed.

My father and mother both grew up in our village. They had an arranged marriage and unfortunately there was drama right from the beginning. My father's parents never got along with my parents. They didn't give as much as a scrap of clothing to cover us. My mother's parents took care of us as best they could, although they too were poor.

So, when my brother and I were very little, my parents asked for their part of the family property and moved out on their own. This was highly unusual and it caused quite a stir. Everyone in our village lives in joint families, with all the generations together.

My father was a good man. He was completely frank with everyone. He was known throughout the area for his integrity. He loved me a lot, much more than my mother did. He was always very tender with me. My father was passionate about education. He would work the whole day in the fields and then study at night to better himself. As there was no electricity in our village, he had to study by the light of an oil lamp. It was difficult, but he managed to learn some reading and writing. His great passion in life was to teach and share knowledge with others.

One day the government decided to establish a school in a neighboring village, but they couldn't find anyone to take the responsibility of managing it. They searched all over that village for a responsible person to look after the school. Then they heard about my father.
When they found him and gave the responsibility to him, he established the school near our house.

My father worked at the school as a substitute teacher as well as a principal and a guard. He also cleaned the school and made food for the students. His salary for all these responsibilities was just Rs. 800 ($80) per month. He was a humble person, willing to do whatever was necessary to keep the school running. The government had provided a teacher from the city. Whenever the teacher was absent, my father would teach us. I made it to grade three, but as the education system was not good, I didn't know yet how to read and write.

We were a happy family, but when I was seven years old, my father became very ill. I don't know what disease he had, because he was never taken to a doctor. I think now that he may have had cancer. At first, he had some problems with his vision, then slowly he started to get sick, with headaches, fevers and a rattling cough. He didn't have deep pain. He just became weaker and weaker.

The villagers called *jhankris* (traditional doctors) and priests, and they just kept sacrificing animals and not giving him any modern medicine. For six months they went on like that. They tried their best, but they wasted that time. No one ever took my father to the hospital. Finally, a person from another village brought some medicine and tried to feed it to him, but it was too late. He couldn't swallow it.

I can still hear my father's voice, talking to my grandfather just before he died. He told my grandfather and the villagers gathered around that his children would be in a bad way when he died, so please take care of them. He knew that without him around we would face many problems and dangers, but there was nothing he could do about it. He told my mother to find and marry another man like him after his death.

My mother cried day and night during my father's illness, but she didn't know how to help him. She spent the last days wailing and throwing herself upon my father, begging him, "Please wake up!" Three or four women had to hold her back.

I watched all this silently from the corner. I didn't cry or wail or throw myself on the floor. The house was already full of crying and yelling, so instead I tried to be very good and quiet. I thought if I was perfectly quiet and good, maybe things would be alright. But of course, no amount of good behavior can stop someone from dying. That night my father left us.

Chapter 2

The week after my father died, we used up all our food. There was a three-day funeral ceremony called a *ghewa*. In Tamang tradition, we invited over two hundred people from the community, and we had to buy and prepare a banquet for them.

During the three-day ceremony, everyone was eating and drinking, some people were fighting, and some singing. The wild party atmosphere felt wrong to me. My life as I knew it was over. There was a big black hole in my life where my father used to be. I felt like everyone and everything should stop and be quiet to match my sorrow, not fighting and singing.

There were huge expenses for the ghewa. It was more elaborate than a marriage ceremony. Six different times the week after my father's death, we had to hire a priest to do a ceremony. The priests would make food for my father, put his clothes on a harvesting tray, and make a doll in his likeness. Then they would call his soul and feed him the best foods, like eggs. They threw all that food away after the ceremony, believing it had been eaten by my father and was no longer edible.

We made huge barrels of wine out of corn for everyone, using all the food stores that we had. I became very worried, watching the cupboards becoming emptier by the day.

As soon as people heard about my father's death, they started talking about the school, who would get to take it over and profit from it. Before my father had taken his last breath, my uncle was already talking about putting the school in his name so he could get the money from the government. Thankfully my father had a good friend from the next village, who also managed a school. That man helped us to put the school in my mother's name, rather than my uncle's.

Before my father died, we were not rich, but we had everything we needed. We had a house and enough fields to grow our food. We had three buffalo, a mother and two of her calves. When my father died, my mom had to sell the mother buffalo in order to pay for the ghewa. My brother and I dropped out of school to work with my mother in the fields so we could all survive.

And then, slowly, things began to fall apart.

My mother was twenty-nine years old, still a beautiful young woman, and many men approached her for marriage. About a year after my father died, she moved out of the house and into a shepherd's hut, a half hour walk from the main house. She took one of our two remaining buffalo with her.

At first she would just go to the hut in the daytime to feed the buffalo, and come back at night to make dinner, and sleep at the house with us. But then slowly, after a few months, she started taking her clothes up there, and then her cooking utensils. Then she would come home only once every three or four days. Finally, she settled herself into that place and rarely came home at all.

I was heartbroken, but at eight years old, I was powerless to stop it. No matter how much I begged and cried, my mother would not come back to us.

People in the village started to gossip about my mother's behavior. They would say to me, "Oh, we saw that your mother was with someone". I doubted that it was true, until one evening when I went up to the hut to visit her. I was feeling really lonely and desperate to stay with her. Then it started to get dark and I was afraid to walk home by myself. I begged my mother to let me stay with her, but she harshly refused me. She sent me back alone, scolding me. My heart crumbled to dust.

That made me start to believe what the villagers were saying about my mother seeing other men. Why else would she have refused to let me stay with her, when it was so late and dark, and I was so small? Sometimes, I saw my mother around the village, talking to different guys. I never said anything, to her or to anyone else.

In the early days, when my mother was still coming home every few days, she was always in an aggressive mood. She just wasn't the same person as before. She had no kind words for us. She took no joy in cooking for us, or in working the fields together. She would just hit us and shout at us.

I understand now that my mother was depressed or suffering from a mental breakdown. But as a child, I didn't understand why she turned away from me. I wondered all the time, what had I done to make her stop loving me? I ached for my mother's love, and I missed my father painfully. A deep sadness began to grow in me.

For my brother and I to survive on our own was difficult, to say the least. There was some food in our home, like corn and millet, but that millet needed to be ground and cooked. We didn't have those skills. Since we didn't know how to cook for ourselves, we would just roam around the village every night to see if anyone had extra food that they could give us, or if we could stay the night at their houses. I was constantly in a state of anxiety. I dreaded begging for scraps from our neighbors' tables. I felt embarrassed to be so needy, because they were poor people too, and often had nothing to share.

On one occasion, there was a nasty incident. Some villagers claimed that my mother had been sleeping with this guy in the village. I had seen her with other men, but not with that man. She went to her parents' house to rally her father and uncles to defend her. The villagers called a meeting at the school and they brought the guy that people said my mother was sleeping with. There was a lot of shouting and accusing, a huge fuss, but in the end nothing happened. No one would admit to seeing anything.

About a year after my mother moved to the shepherd's hut, some men from another village came to our house, bringing me the gold jewelry that my father had given my mother when they married. According to our tradition, when a woman remarries, she must return her dowry from the previous marriage to the family. That was how I learned that my mother had gotten remarried.

Chapter 3

When I finally met my new stepfather, I was relieved to discover that he was a nice guy. He was ten years younger than my mother, so he was only about twenty at that time. I loved when I was allowed to stay at my mother and stepfather's house, as a family. I didn't often get to stay at their house, because my stepfather's parents didn't want me and my brother around, but when I did, it was wonderful.

A lot of difficult things seemed to happen every day. I grew very thin, and my hair became thin also. I was always dirty and ragged, because no one was taking care of me, or teaching me how to care for myself.

I do have a few good memories, like when I could get work from richer people to work in their fields. My brother and I would go and pick grains all day. They would give us just 20 or 30 rupees (25 cents), but it was a lot for us, because we didn't have any money at that time. Then I would go to the shop and buy special foods, different from what we had at home. We usually just ate coarse corn and millet, but when we earned money, we could buy noodles or beaten rice, or even cookies. I would bring that special food home, and put it on plates, and then I would call my brother and we would sit together and eat it. We always made a big occasion out of it.

After my mother remarried, my grandfather decided that my brother and I should not be alone in the home, so he sent us to live with my uncle and aunt. This was my father's brother and his wife. We stayed almost two months with them but they didn't behave well towards us at all.

One evening there was a big fight. We had all been in the field working, but before it got too late, my aunt sent my brother to get water and light the fire. But he was a child. He liked to play with his friends. So he went to play and didn't do his chores. My aunt became enraged and began beating him savagely. She had her legs wrapped around his chest and was crushing him. My uncle had to pull them apart. That night my brother ran away, back to our family home. He didn't come back to my aunt and uncle's house after that.

I was so worried about my brother, living on his own at just ten years old. I was afraid of my uncle and aunt, who were always shouting and often slapping me. I had to fake a smile and choke back my tears because otherwise they would punish me for crying.

While I was living with my uncle and aunt, my job was to care for their baby. At one point, my mother came and wanted to take me to visit her brother. I was afraid I would be punished, but I went with my mother anyway. When my uncle saw me leaving, he called me back, saying they needed me to take care of the baby. I was torn about what to do. I loved spending time with my mother. I hadn't seen her for almost a month. I decided to go with her to visit her side of the family for a few days. After that, I decided it wouldn't be safe to go back to my aunt and uncle's house. So, I went back to our family home, and my brother and I settled in to living there alone.

Things continued, the same but a little worse.

Every night we would go house to house asking for food. It was hard to find every lunch, every dinner. We would play with our friends in the afternoons, but then when night fell, the other kids all went inside their own houses. Each house was bright with burning fires in the kitchen but ours was cold and dark. There were spoiled foods in our kitchen, crops being eaten by rats because we didn't know how to cook or store them properly. Other family's gardens were green with vegetables, but our garden was yellow with dust.

We used to take our grain to other people's houses as our contribution to the meal. Jesika is a relative of mine and her home was near to my mother's new house. After my mother remarried, I sometimes spent the night at Jesika's house. Her family was poor, but food was prepared in their home. They were kind to us.

Because I didn't know how to take care of myself, I frequently had lice, dirty clothes, and illnesses. Once a relative saw the lice in my head and cut all my hair off with a blade. I was so embarrassed! My hair seemed to take forever to grow back. Other children also got lice, but their mothers would take the time to comb and wash their hair. Having a shaven head marked me as a motherless child.

My mom got pregnant immediately after her marriage and had a daughter, Dipti. Unfortunately, baby Dipti became very sick in her first year, so my mother had even less time for us.

My brother refused to go to my stepfather's house, and he wouldn't talk to my mother at all. He was furious that she had gotten married without telling us, and that she had left us to raise ourselves alone. It is true that it wasn't normal. In the village, families live with many generations together -parents, grandparents, uncles, aunts and cousins. But I wasn't angry with my mother. I was just hungry for whatever love I could get from her.

That year after my mother got married, really bad things started to happen. Sometimes when I was alone in the house, male relatives tried to sleep with me and touch my body. I didn't tell anyone about it. To this day, I have never told anyone the names of the two men who abused me. Those men were, in other ways, the most loving people in my life. They showed me a lot of affection. They gave me things that I wanted and needed. I trusted them because they were my own relatives.

I was desperate for affection and care and I didn't know enough to stop what was happening. I didn't understand anything about sex, and I didn't even know what they were doing was wrong. Yet somehow I still felt ashamed, so I couldn't tell anyone what was happening. Also, there was really no one to tell.

One of the hardest things was that my brother and I began to grow apart. He started following the wrong people. When he was twelve or thirteen, he began hanging around with traffickers, playing cards and drinking alcohol with them. My brother is the kind of person who always does what others tell him to do. The hurt of our father's death and our mother's abandonment created, in both of us, a wound that would not heal. It made us willing to do anything to get the love we craved, to be accepted. The boys my brother was following were very broken people. They had forgotten their true identity as human beings. They wouldn't leave any girl over the age of ten alone.

With everything that was happening, I felt the storm clouds gathering around me. The constant, low-grade worry that I had felt ever since my father died, changed to a deep foreboding.

Chapter 4

When I was a child, families in our village would often send their daughters to work in brothels in India. Sadly, this practice continues to this day. Some girls leave willingly, tricked by the false promises of traffickers. Some go with the hope of earning money and solving the problems of their parents and brothers. Some are sold by family members, blinded by the dream of becoming rich. Some go to avoid forced marriage, or they are sold by their own husbands after a child marriage.

Girls would leave or be taken from the village. Then, after a few days we would hear that they had made their way to cities like Delhi, Kolkata and Mumbai, and were in some known or unknown brothel owner's hands. At that point, the parents would become angry with their daughters and with the traffickers. They might even damage the house of the trafficker if they knew his identity.

But later, when the girls started sending money home, the families would receive it happily, apparently forgetting their anger and concern. They would enjoy the money without asking where their daughter was, how she was doing, and what kind of job she had to do to earn that money.

People in the village who had sent a daughter to India built new houses and got new roofs. You could tell who had sold a daughter or wife by the condition of their house and roof. The system of trafficking had become completely normalized in our village. No one questioned it. As a young child, I understood that most girls from the village were sent to India to work. But I had no idea what kind of work they did.

I remember many girls coming back from India, including several of my own aunts and cousins. My father had two sisters and they were both trafficked as teenagers. When they came back, they were older, and had gotten married. Like all the women who came back from India, my aunts came bearing gifts, new clothes, chocolates, and fancy foods like we never had in the village. They wore gold earrings. Their hands were clean and smooth, not like the hands of the village women who worked in the fields. We were quite amazed by their smooth hands and their wealth. It was easy for traffickers to trick the villagers because we were naive about the rest of the world. The wealth from abroad seemed incredible to us.

When I was eleven, my friend Anisha's parents made her go with an aunt to work in India, because they were so poor and they had eight other children. People in the village didn't use birth control, so every year they would have another child. Anisha was the eldest daughter of her family, and it was becoming very hard for her parents to feed all the kids. They saw the money that other families in the village were receiving from their daughters in the brothels, so as soon as Anisha turned eleven, they made her go. She cried very hard, for many days, and begged her parents not to send her, but they were deaf to her cries. Their minds were already hardened. I never saw Anisha again.

Seeing this happening to Anisha, and to other girls my age, I became very afraid. I knew that I had no one to protect me. I was an obvious target.

When I turned eleven, boys from a neighboring village began coming to take me by force for marriage. They chased me relentlessly. My mother and stepfather were unable to stop it. I had to hide the entire day in the jungle to evade them. I could come home only after it was dark. Even when I was sick, I had to go into the jungle to hide from those boys. It was exhausting.

Sometimes I would play by myself in the forest. Sometimes I would meet a shepherd and chat with him. Usually, I just collected firewood or herbs to bring home in the evening.

One day, after working in the fields all day with my mother, I decided to take a bath and wash my clothes. My mother told me to go into the jungle and take a bath there, because she feared the boys would come soon. But I was tired and irritable and didn't listen to my mother. I said "Today I want to take my bath here with you and wash my clothes with you. I don't want to go in the jungle. Maybe the boys will not come today".

My mother agreed and we both stood under the tap to shower and wash our clothes. It was an outdoor tap behind the house. My baby sister was asleep beside us. My mother had just started to wash my hair when the boys suddenly appeared beside the house and saw us bathing. My mother scolded me, "If you had obeyed me and gone in the jungle, this would not have happened!"

The boys didn't leave as we finished washing our clothes and bathing. They just stood there watching. My heart was racing. My mother told me to pick up my baby sister. "Walk slowly in front of me," she whispered, "and when we are behind the house and they can't see you, run fast and I will keep them from following you. Leave your sister in the house and run into the jungle. I will come get you when the boys are gone".

I did exactly as she told me. I ran into the jungle, faster and farther than I had ever run before. I could see the boys from my hiding place in the jungle. They waited a long time, searching everywhere for me.

The next day, my mother sent me to stay in my grandparent's home, which was in another village where the boys did not do such things. I stayed there for about two months but my grandparents could not keep me forever, and I needed to work to keep our family farm going.

When I returned home, the boys continued to menace me. I still had to hide every day in the jungle. They always made up different reasons for hanging around our house. Sometimes they would ask if we had some alcohol to drink. Sometimes they came to offer cigarettes, or to collect money for *pujas* (religious celebrations).

Once, a trafficker saw me hiding in the jungle, and asked "Do you want to go with me, to the place where all your sisters go? You can make a lot of money there". When I refused, he said, "Then I will show the boys where you are hiding and they will take you for marriage, you foolish girl!"

My stepfather and mother were in financial trouble. My baby sister had been very sick that year, and there were medical bills. They owed money to the men who built their house, and they needed to eat twice a day. They were in distress and I couldn't do anything. I wanted to help them by working in the fields, but the boys never left me any time to work properly. I was conflicted about what to do, how to help them.

23

I know now that my childhood should have been a time to play and be loved and cared for by my family. How could I have supported my own parents? Eleven years old is not the time for getting a job to support your family.

Chapter 5

Our village had no rule of law. Everyone lived according to ancient traditions. If someone was murdered, the killer rarely got punished. The killer would just leave the community and go live in another place for a few years. When he eventually returned, the event which had happened years before was forgotten. During certain festivals and ceremonies, people would be killed or beaten. Punishment would be meted out in the next festival or ceremony. The friends and relatives of the murdered or beaten people would bring a mob of their own people to take revenge.

If boys from one village took a girl from another village to force her into marriage, then people from the girl's village would go and take girls from the village that had taken her. Revenge would be taken, but that did not help the little girls forced into marriage at all. They were soon forgotten, after revenge was taken on their behalf. Once they were forced into marriage, they had no choice but to stay in the marriage.

On the rare occasions when the police came into the community, no one would open their mouth. People were scared of the police and didn't know anything about laws or rights.

When I was a young girl, my dream was to study and then later to get married. People used to tell me I should go to India instead. They said if I went to India, then I would be beautiful and rich, and wouldn't need to work in the fields.

In the spring of 2006, just before I turned twelve, some traffickers came to ask my mother to give me to them, so they could take me to India. I was unsure about what to do, whether I should agree to go to India, to work and earn money for my family. I was worried about my mother and stepfather's economic condition. I was afraid of being forced to marry an old man. My brother was getting into trouble and was no longer there for me. Everyone in the village seemed to be pressuring me to go to India. No one was protecting me or advising me not to go. Of course, I had no idea what it really meant to work in India. I didn't know girls were forced into prostitution, or even what prostitution was.

The village was deteriorating day by day. It seemed there were no families without a daughter in India. Some families had two, three, and four daughters working in Indian brothels. Many young men remained single because there were no young women for them to marry. Nobody raised their voice against this system. Everyone either went along with it or was actively involved in it.

After thinking through all these things, I decided to go to India. My reasoning was that if I stayed in the village and got married, I wouldn't be able to do anything to help my parents. Everyone said that I could earn good money in India. One of my aunts was already there, and I figured I could stay with her and she would take care of me. Perhaps my strongest motivation was that I was worn down from all the hiding and constant fear. I was ready to do anything to make that feeling go away.

And so, when one of my uncles met me in the jungle and told me that he could take me to my aunt in India, I said yes. He told me that we would be leaving later that very day, in the middle of the night. He warned me not to tell anyone because if other people found out, they wouldn't allow me to go, and then I wouldn't be able to earn money to help my family.

At 3:00 am, I made my way secretly to a nearby forest. At first I thought that I was going to meet up with just that one uncle, but there was another girl there, Laxmi, and three more men who were also traffickers. These men were well known to me. They were Tamang, and distantly related to me. Laxmi was a year older than me. Like me, she had a typically Tamang appearance, with light skin, a round face, straight black hair, and wide-set eyes.

They brought different clothes for us called *kurtas* - a long shirt and trousers. They had us change out of our traditional Nepali clothes into the kurtas. They told us to hurry, so we could get out of the village before anybody woke up and found out that we were escaping.

We traveled by way of the forest to Kathmandu, walking that whole night and two days.

I remember climbing so many hills that my legs were burning. I began to wish I hadn't left the village. As it was becoming light, I turned back to look at my village. But I couldn't see it anymore. My eyes filled with tears.

I realized then that I had made a mistake, but those four men were not about to let me turn back.

On the evening of the second day, we reached a mountain from which we could see the city of Kathmandu, the capital of Nepal. I was a young village girl who had never gone anywhere beyond the next small town. I saw this big city and thought that it was the whole world. It was so large that I couldn't take it all in at once. I was speechless and overwhelmed.

My heart was truly not at peace. All I could think about was my family and village, when or if I would ever see them again. I was scared that something bad was about to happen and full of a sickening regret for my own role in the situation. As a child, I believed that everything that happened was my full responsibility. I couldn't see that I had been caught up in a large and complex web of international organized crime.

When we got closer to Kathmandu, we got into a van. Immediately I fell asleep, exhausted from the long walk, slumped in a trafficker's lap. He woke me up after many hours as we had reached our destination. It was nighttime. The men were paying our fares when I heard the van driver saying that he wouldn't need a fare for me, because I looked like a small child.

We went to a building which must have been a hotel. Our room had three beds and a toilet. We washed our faces and then the men took us down for dinner. For me, everything was strange and different - the hotel, traveling by bus and car, and the food - so I didn't eat much. While we were at dinner, I saw someone coming from inside a box and saying something and then going away. This, I learned, was television.

I was feeling more and more scared and disoriented, seeing so many strange things for the first time in my life. In the morning they moved us to another hotel because someone had recognized them. They told us that if they were recognized, we would all be put in jail.

Two of the guys went outside and brought new clothes and shoes for us. That night they started making nasty jokes, threatening to make us switch beds, to sleep in their beds with them. Laxmi and I held each other in fear, but nothing happened that night.

At 3:00 or 4:00 in the morning. they woke us up. The men phoned somebody who picked us up and took us to the bus station. The plan was for us all to take the same bus but to pretend we were traveling separately and didn't know each other. On the bus ride, I got car sick and vomited a lot. I had never ridden in a car or bus before coming to Kathmandu.

On the bus, one of the traffickers coached me, saying "If the police ask where you are going, tell them you are going to India to see your mother. Say that I am your brother and that we are going together to meet our mother".

After traveling the whole day by bus, we reached a new place at night. They took us to a hotel, where we met a man from my village and an aunt of mine, Luma. She seemed distressed, rather than happy to see me, which I didn't understand. Luma urged me to go back to the village but did not explain why, or tell me anything about what awaited me.

Before I even had the chance to answer Luma, the men began talking about money, just outside our room. The man from my village gave 40,000 rupees to each of the four traffickers, about $1600 US dollars in total.

That was the price for two girls' lives.

After some time, we were taken back to the bus station. The men who had taken us from the village came to say goodbye and then they left, back to the village. I was not fond of those guys, and they had been very nasty in the hotel room the night before. But when they left, it felt as if the thin rope connecting me to my home stretched even thinner. I felt cold and empty, watching them go. I wished that I too was going back home.

The bus drove all night and it went very fast, now that we were no longer on winding mountain roads. I don't remember a border crossing, but there must have been one, because in the early morning we reached our first destination in India. I felt a little spark of hope then. I wondered what kind of work I would be doing in India, and how things would be for me.

Chapter 6

Two women were waiting to meet us at the bus station. My aunt told me to go with them and that she would join me later. The women took us to a small house and told us we would be staying there for a while. We went inside, where a man and woman and another girl from our village were eating their lunch. They gave food to us too, and the two ladies left us there. I thought that my aunt would come and take me with her later, but she never came.

We spent eight days in that room, never once seeing the sunlight. Whenever somebody came to the house, they would hide us under the bed. For the first few days, I cried continuously, calling out for my mother. The adults slept on the bed and the girls had to sleep on the floor. They gave us no blankets or bed sheets, and we were cold at night. We couldn't sleep due to the cold and the mosquito bites.

I began to understand that something was very wrong about the situation. Nothing was as I had expected. The couple fought constantly. They didn't give us enough food. My hair was long when I arrived, but the woman cut it very short. Eight days trapped inside that room was a very dark time for me. I was a village child, used to working outside all day and running freely, wherever I wanted. I thought a lot about my mother. Whenever I would say or think the word 'mother', my eyes would fill with tears. Those eight days were like eight years to me. I could never get a full breath.

On the eighth day, Laxmi's aunt called. She said that she would come the next day with new clothes for us. When she came with the clothes, I did not get a good feeling. Laxmi's aunt was not a nice person. That evening, the woman in the house suddenly ordered us to put on the new clothes that Laxmi's aunt had brought. Our own clothes were filthy by then from the long journey and from eight days sleeping on the floor. She said that the police were coming into the building to check something. I had no idea what they were checking, but I had been raised to be afraid and suspicious of police.

The next day, the woman took us outside, where Laxmi's aunt was waiting for us, and we were sent off with her. The couple hadn't been giving us enough food, so we were quite hungry. We told Laxmi's aunt that we didn't want to stay there anymore. She agreed to take us far from that place. The three of us got in a taxi and drove for two or three hours.

When the taxi stopped, two girls were there to meet us. This place, we learned, was the city of Kolkata. It was an enormous city of fifteen million souls, buzzing with activity. Everyone seemed to be rushing around, on every possible kind of vehicle - bicycles, cars, rickshaws, bicycle rickshaws, autorickshaws, and wooden carts like we had in the village, which men were pulling by hand. Laxmi's aunt told us to go with the two girls, and they took us on foot to our next destination.

We walked on busy streets, then smaller roads, then narrow lanes, then even smaller alleyways, just wide enough to walk single file. The further we walked, the worse the area seemed to get. There was open sewage running down the middle of the alleys, and the smell was horrible. Old ladies and tiny children were sleeping on the sidewalk on pieces of cardboard. There was garbage everywhere and the buildings seemed to be about to collapse. Though it was daytime, it seemed dark there, partly from the heavy smog and partly from the narrowness of the alleyways. There were lots of girls and young women standing in groups everywhere, and in each building, more girls were sitting and standing.

This was the Sonagachi red light area. Kolkata's largest and most profitable red light area, home to a captive population of over 20,000 women and children.

The house where they took us was in appalling condition. Our room was more like a hole than a room. There was a small bed inside it. As the house was owned by a large family, and we were four girls in the room, we took turns sleeping in the bed, under the bed, on the floor next to the bed, in the house owner's room, or just outside the room. Since I was the smallest, I was usually under the bed.

For the next five days, I was almost always hidden under the bed except in the morning to go to the bathroom, because I looked very young, especially after having my hair cut. We Nepalis are generally quite small, and I had poor nutrition as a child. so I was unusually small for my age.

The days I spent in that room in Sonagachi were a dark time. It made the eight days I had just spent in a room seem not so bad. While hiding under the bed, I slept as much as I could, and I daydreamed about my village and family. I would have given anything for a long day working in the fields, or even hiding in the forest collecting herbs. Those experiences, which had seemed quite difficult at the time, were suddenly all that I wanted. The time passed slowly.

Some of my female relatives and neighbors from the village heard that I had come to Kolkata and came to see me. After five days, my aunt Luma came and urged me once again to go back to the village. "I don't want to go back home yet, but I want to live with you," I told her.

I still didn't know the truth of the situation, and I would have felt very ashamed to go back home empty-handed, not having earned a single rupee to help my family. As desperately as I wanted to go home and to see my mother and brother, I knew there was nothing there for me except a child marriage and a life of struggle.

Luma insisted that I needed to go home immediately. She was quite forceful about it. She told Laxmi and me to be ready at 5:00 pm that evening. She promised to put us on a train back to Nepal. I began to feel a little hopeful, and relieved that my ordeal in India was coming to an end. But that evening, instead of my aunt Luma, it was Laxmi's aunt who came to the house to pick us up.

Out loud, in front of the others, she said the same thing my aunt had said. "You girls are too young to be here. You need to go home. I will help you get out of here".

But then she whispered in my ear, "Don't worry, we are not really going back to the village. We are going to another place, much better than here. You will love it there, I promise".

The other girls warned us not to go with Laxmi's aunt, but they would not explain why. So she took us, telling everyone that she was just taking us to buy shoes, and then sending us back to the village. She took us in a rickshaw to a shoe shop, where she did indeed buy new shoes for us. But then, instead of going to the train station, we met up with another couple, who took us to another building in the red light area. This building was decrepit on the outside, but bigger and a little better inside than the place where I had been kept under a bed for the last five days. There were three bedrooms, two toilets and a kitchen on the top floor. There was a Nepali servant who cleaned the rooms and cooked the food.

There was also a young boy living there, studying in grade nine. His parents were the man and woman who we met on the way there. The Nepali servant prepared dinner for us. When it got late, the parents left us and the boy there with the Nepali servant, saying they would come to meet us the next day.

"Stay well, eat well and get big soon," they told us.

What an odd thing to say, I thought.

The months that followed were a strange time. It was a huge improvement on the eight days in a room, and the five days under a bed. All we had to do was eat and sleep, and grow older and bigger so our periods would start, so we wouldn't look like little children. For the first time in my life, I had enough to eat. I slept a lot, lulled into a false sense of safety. Everything was done by the Nepali servant. They even sent a tutor to teach us some Bengali and English.

I really don't know why they bothered to hire a tutor for us. Was it to distract us, to keep us occupied so we wouldn't try to try to escape, or cry and scream for help? Or was it to teach us some languages commonly spoken there, so we could communicate with customers, so we wouldn't seem like the naive village girls that we actually were? I think maybe they wanted to convince themselves, and the outside world that they were doing right by us.

They fed us well because they wanted us to grow up quickly, to start our periods. We still weren't allowed to go outside, which was hard for me as a child of the village, who had roamed freely in the forest her whole life. They forbade us even to look out the windows or go up on the roof. When the servant went out to buy food, he would lock the door from the outside. Kolkata was much hotter and more humid than my mountain home in Nepal. Between the heat and being locked in, I found it hard to breathe.

The couple would come to visit their son from time to time, and Laxmi's aunt used to visit her sometimes, but Luma never came to see me. She called me occasionally on the phone. When she called, she sounded sad and distant, which made me feel lonelier than ever.

Every day was the same. Our daily routine was to wake up and take a bath, eat breakfast, watch TV, eat lunch and sleep for several hours, wake up again to watch more TV or play *Karam*, a board game. At 4:00 in the afternoon, we had a snack. If the tutor came, we would study with him for a few hours. then watch yet more TV, eat dinner and go to sleep.

Looking back on it, there were many signs that something was wrong, but I was too naive to read them. I had been caught in a very complicated trap, cleverly designed to make me come willingly to India and to keep me cooperating until it was too late. From the four men who took me from the village, to the couple at this house, to the various men and women involved in our transit, at least eleven people had already been involved in trafficking us.

In that house, I learned to write some English letters and to do some simple math. With regular meals, I grew taller and less scrawny. Still I knew nothing about the things that were happening all around me, or the reason I had been brought to Kolkata. When the boy asked us what we were doing there and why we had come, we told him that we had come to study and we would soon go back home, because that was what the traffickers told us.

Nine months passed. The days ran together because every day was much the same. It seemed that this was my new life in India, and I got used to it. It really wasn't so bad. But then one day my period came, and everything changed.

Chapter 7

Halfway across the world, Don Gerred was feeling conflicted about what to do. Don was a thirty-eight- year- old lawyer working as a narcotics prosecutor in Western Pennsylvania. He and his wife Lori were raising three little girls. They were very involved at their church, and with various social causes. Their lives were happy and very busy.

Don was a quietly intense kind of person. He had a wry, and slightly dark sense of humor. He came across as very professional, reserved and not the emotional type. But underneath the cool exterior, his heart burned hotly for justice. He felt deeply the pain of others.

Don enjoyed the camaraderie of the narcotics task force. He discovered through that job that he was a bit of an adrenaline junkie. But still it felt like something was missing in his life. He felt called to do something about the worst injustices of the world. He longed to use his skills for something with a bigger impact, something that could permanently change people's lives for the better.

After months of job-searching and soul-searching, Don decided to accept a position at International Justice Mission - IJM - leading a legal team at one of their field offices. The office was literally on the other side of the world, in Kolkata.

IJM was an international organization which partnered with local justice systems to end violence against people living in poverty. They rescued people from slavery, and pursued justice for victims through the courts of their own countries. The Kolkata field office was specifically focused on rescuing young girls from slavery in brothels.

The job felt like a good fit to Don. He wanted to work in a close-knit team, with a big mission, and he had always liked heist movies. He guessed that the job would involve plenty of action and adrenaline. Don felt hopeful that in Kolkata, he would be able to have the positive impact he longed to have in the lives of the most vulnerable.

And so, in May 2006, Don and Lori left behind everything they had ever known and moved across the world to Kolkata. Their daughters were seven, six and one year old.

The flights to India took over twenty-four hours. The family arrived at Kolkata airport at 3:00 in the morning, jet-lagged and disheveled, with piles of luggage and three exhausted and crying little girls. There were crowds of people in the airport, even at that late hour, and many more waiting outside. It was unnaturally hot for such a late hour, and there was a faint smell of wood fires, manure, spice, exhaust and burning garbage. Driving to their hotel took over an hour, through the most crowded and chaotic city Don had ever seen. He felt overwhelmed and a little worried. But it was definitely too late to turn back.

Adjusting to life in Kolkata did turn out to be hard. The Kolkata field office was quite new. The team was not as cohesive as Don had hoped. Some key positions had not yet been filled. There were ambitious targets for the number of rescue raids. The targets were an internal goal of how many trafficking victims IJM thought the team should be able to rescue each month. However, the pieces were not in place yet to conduct successful raids.

A year later, the team had rescued very few girls, and the family was still struggling to adjust to life in Kolkata. Don and Lori tried to find a good school for their daughters, with no success. The local school was extremely under-resourced. There were sixty children in each class, teachers who were often absent, and rats. Then they found what seemed to be a better school, but it turned out to be a Hindu fundamentalist school. There, the girls were branded as 'untouchable', harshly treated by teachers and bullied by other kids because they were foreigners and the family was Christian. In the end, Lori decided to home-school the girls.

Kolkata itself was a challenge - a city of fifteen million without enough roads or services. The crowds, air pollution and noise pollution were overwhelming, especially for someone from a small city in Western Pennsylvania.

There were some things about Kolkata that Don enjoyed. People were very industrious and warm, resilient and uncomplaining. Friends and neighbors would often drop by unannounced for long visits. There was a lot of history and culture in the city. Though many buildings were old and stained with damp, everything was colorfully and intricately decorated.

The winter weather wasn't too bad, but May and June brought temperatures of 115 degrees or more with intense humidity. The monsoon rains, which come in July, brought some relief from the heat, but then the streets were repeatedly flooded with two feet of sewage-tainted water. There wasn't enough green space for the girls to play outdoors and enjoy nature. There was a lot of staring and pushing and cutting in line.

More than these physical discomforts, Don was shocked by the amount of poverty, and by the fact that so many people seemed to just walk on by, blind to the suffering of others. The streets in many parts of the city were blanketed with pavement dwellers, families living under tarps by the side of the road or under bridges. Their houses were woven together from bamboo, or scraps of tin and cardboard, built with great effort and care, but useless against the monsoon rains. Children ran amongst the busy traffic, begging or hawking gum, flowers or fruit. The city's five red light areas were overflowing with neglected and exploited children. Few people seemed to notice or care.

In 2007, after a year in India, Don and Lori decided that life in Kolkata was just too hard on their family. The office was failing and there was talk of it being shut down. They needed to go home. Don got an offer for a job in Denver on a Saturday. He decided he would tell IJM the following Monday. But on Sunday, his boss - the Director of IJM South Asia - called and said they had decided to make a change in leadership. He asked Don if he would take over the Kolkata office. If Don's boss had waited another day to make the offer, it would have been too late.

As soon as Don took over as Field Director, he began looking for a Lead Investigator. After a few months, he hired Victor Lacey, a highly decorated former U.S. Marine and experienced narcotics detective. Vic was responsible for identifying the places where underage girls were being sold. He mapped out brothel buildings, and gathered information on the traffickers, pimps, madams and brothel managers. Whenever possible, these criminals were arrested as part of the raid, and prosecuted to the fullest extent of the law.

Don and Vic recruited and trained a team of operatives. These were local guys, whose job it was to go into the brothels posing as customers, wearing hidden cameras. A group of three or four operatives went each night into the brothels, looking for new girls and minors. They met with the same girls each time they visited, so the manager wouldn't become suspicious, but they were always on the lookout for new girls. They brought the film footage to Vic, who used it to create a detailed map of the building. Vic would compare each night's footage with footage from past nights to determine if there were new girls at that brothel.

The operatives' job was critical to conducting a successful raid. It was also incredibly dangerous. Many operatives have been beaten or even killed by traffickers in the course of their work. It was also an emotionally taxing job, to see so much suffering night after night. It was a delicate matter to buy time with a trafficked girl, convince her that you just wanted to talk, and get information that could help with a rescue without letting the girl know that a raid was about to happen. Every time the operatives returned to the same brothel, and every minute they spent there, the risk became higher.

The operatives talked to the girls about ordinary things, to build trust. For example, they might pretend they were having problems with their girlfriend or wife and just needed to talk. In the midst of a casual chat, they snuck in questions like "Where you are from? How long have you been here? How old are you?"

Don spent a long time interviewing and choosing the right guys for the job. Once they were on the job, he made sure they got lots of counseling, spiritual and emotional support, and breaks between visits to brothels. He looked for men with strong nerves, who could handle the extreme danger and constant fear of the job. He looked for emotionally mature guys, who wouldn't be tempted to have inappropriate relationships with the girls. He insisted that the operatives' body cameras were always on, and that they were always in pairs, never alone.

Don would have loved to participate in raids himself but as a 6'4" blonde man, he was never going to blend in. As a very obvious foreigner, his presence would have attracted unwanted attention and that could jeopardize the next raid. So he focused on the preparations behind the scenes. He laid the traps.

As the new boss, Don took a little getting used to. He was very tall, very white, and very intense. People were scared of him until they got to know him. His quirky sense of humor helped to ease any awkwardness. Everyone needed to laugh and goof around in the IJM office, because it was such a dark job otherwise.

By the spring of 2008, all the hard work began to show results. A strong team was in place, fully trained, and working smoothly together. After a few successful raids, the team set their sights on a brothel in the Mahishidal red light area. This brothel was known for trafficking young Nepali girls. The brothel manager and the brothel owner, Nakul Bera, were notoriously violent. Bera was known to personally rape new arrivals. On one occasion he beat a girl to death with a club for disobedience.

Don and Vic discovered that a girl of thirteen was being held at the brothel. They decided to plan a raid to rescue her and the other underage girls whose lives were at risk in that place. The first time a raid was scheduled, it had to be called off because someone had tipped off the brothel owners. The leak almost had certainly come from within the police. Police corruption was an enormous problem.

The team tried seven more times to raid the brothel. Finally, on their eighth attempt, they succeeded. They rescued the thirteen-year-old and three other young girls. But, as the IJM team was searching the brothel for more girls, Bera and his goons were chasing the rest of the girls across a field with wooden clubs.

Grateful for the four girls they saved that day, and heartsick for the ones that were chased away, Don got straight back to work, sifting through the ashes, planning the next raid.

Chapter 8

One day, without warning, Laxmi and I were moved to a different place. The lady who managed the house came in the morning with different clothes for us, brightly colored tunics and saris. They were much better than the clothes we had been wearing, which were becoming threadbare. We had come to Kathmandu with just the clothes on our backs, the traffickers bought us one outfit in Kathmandu, and Laxmi's aunt had bought us one other outfit when we moved to Kolkata. Nine and a half months later, all of our clothes were worn out and much too small.

As soon as we put on the new clothes, Laxmi's aunt came to the house and announced, "You are leaving here today".

She took us in a taxi for several hours to the place where we were going to be working. *At last*, I thought happily, *my real life in India is going to begin.*

That place was a brothel run out of a hotel in Haldia, a port town three hours outside Kolkata.
When we arrived at the brothel, it was midday. There were about fifteen other Tamang girls there. I was surprised to see several girls I knew, including Tanu, who lived in the village next to ours.

There were no customers around yet, so Laxmi's aunt took us up to the bedrooms. She showed us our rooms, and then she went outside to organize a meal for us. We ate the meal, and then she taught us how to do our makeup. She showed me how to put on eyeliner, lipstick and powder, things I had never used before.

After a while, some more people came. They were the managers of the brothel. A manager came to call all the girls downstairs. Laxmi's aunt told us to go down with the others and begin our work. God help me, I still didn't know what that work was.

We followed the other girls down to the hotel bar. For a few minutes, we sat on chairs and watched TV. Then a man came into the bar and the manager said something which I couldn't understand. The man sat down on the chair and the manager touched a button which brought a loud noise into the room. As soon as the sound was heard, all the girls got up and went to stand in front of the man. They told me to come with them. The man was at least thirty years old.

After standing there a few seconds, the man looked over all the girls and pointed his finger at me. I was confused about what to do or say. Then the manager gave me a small diary and ordered another girl to give me a condom and a bed sheet. He ordered her to teach me how to deal with the customer. The girl led me to a small room at the back of the hotel. She told me to take the man in there and close the doors from the inside, and to do whatever he asked.

As an innocent child, I obeyed whatever people told me to do. So I did everything as she said. I knew that I had no way to escape. I had heard someone saying that if you disobeyed, they would send you to the worst place, and you would never be able to return to your village.

And so I led the man into that dark, dirty room. The door closed behind us. The man held me down and blood flowed.

I cried out for help but nobody heard me, or if they did hear, they did not come. After a while, the manager knocked on the door and I followed him slowly back downstairs.

Then it happened again. More blood. More crying and calling for help. Still no one came to help me.

The next day was even worse. The wounds of the previous day were painful, but still hour after hour that night, I had to take care of customers. My period had started just a month before. That second day finished with ten customers.

The third day, when the manager came to call all the girls down, I tried to avoid going. But Laxmi's aunt forced me to go down. Like this, one day finished and the next day began. Whichever girl the customer chose would have to give her notebook to the manager. Each girl's notebook, a pouch of contraceptives and a bed sheet was hung on the wall of the hotel. The customer would pay according to how much time he wanted. The manager used to write the number of customers in the girls' notebooks to track how much we earned, but the money was always taken by him, never given to the girls.

Each month, the owners of the girls would come and take half the money we earned. The other half was kept by the brothel managers and the owner of the brothel. If a girl earned $200 in a month, then $100 was taken by her owner, $50 by the brothel managers, and $50 by the house owner. I never saw a single rupee of what I earned.

That brothel was designed for young and new girls to learn the language and to learn to endure the violent and degrading 'work' of prostitution. After breaking girls in, they would move them to the Sonagachi red light area in Kolkata. We were the youngest and thus the most valuable girls. Indian customers liked Nepali girls because of our light skin and our East Asian eye shape. They found us exotic.

.

I wanted to stay with my aunt, but I was told that in order to live with her, I had to be able to speak Hindi fluently and I had to be bigger. I learned to speak Hindi but I remained small.

At first it felt impossibly difficult for me to do that work and to live in that brothel, but somehow I managed to survive it. I had no options. I was always kept in a state of fear and completely powerless. Customers used to complain if they didn't get satisfied, and then there would be more trouble.

After the first few days, when I cried for help and nobody answered. I killed a part of myself and learned to adjust to the work. They didn't call me by my name. They used to call me other names, cruel nicknames that made me feel ugly and worthless. I hated the names they called me, but also I didn't like to hear my real name coming from their mouths. In that place, I wasn't Anjali. I was somebody else, somebody who was able to get through those terrible nights.

In the early days, Laxmi's aunt stayed with us and taught us about the work of prostitution, how to keep the customers happy. She wouldn't allow us to rest in our bedroom for a single minute. No matter how much we begged to rest, she always slapped make-up on our faces and sent us down to the bar.

We were forced to sell our bodies to ten to twenty customers a day. Some were police. Some were truck drivers or day laborers. Some were foreigners, some were Nepali or Indian. Some were my brother's age and some old enough to be my grandfather. Some wanted to spend a night while some wanted to spend thirty minutes. Whoever came, and whatever they wanted, I was just an object for their enjoyment. No one offered to help me. No one ever suggested taking me away from there. No one saw the growing wounds inside me.

The managers and owners would be nice to me if I was able to earn a lot of money. But when I earned only a little money in a month, they scolded me. To get those little kindnesses from them, I had to kill more of myself to earn more money for them. I was hungry for love and starving for any small kindness, so I used to do a lot of things to get their approval.

After eight months, my aunt Luma finally came to see me. She had her own story of betrayal and loss. She was my mother's sister, and when she was very small, my parents married her off to my uncle who was not a good person. He used to beat her savagely. My aunt loved me very much when I was little. She used to send clothes for me when I was in the

49

village. One day my uncle beat her very badly because he wanted to bring another wife into their home and she objected. I was there at the time. I cried a lot, saying, "Please don't beat my aunt".

That very night my aunt ran away from the village. The traffickers took their opportunity to take her into hell that day.

My aunt never scolded me when she learned that I had earned very little money, but Laxmi's aunt scolded and shouted at both of us relentlessly. Possibly, my owner was my aunt and Laxmi's owner was hers.

Our days were filled with unbearable anxiety, dreading the coming night. The customers, managers and owners all wanted to fulfill their desires. They didn't care one tiny bit about me or what I wanted. I was less than human to them. Still, I always tried to make them happy though it was nearly always futile.

The traffickers sometimes brought mothers with young children and pregnant women to the brothel. Some came with a full awareness of the situation. Others like me had no idea what they were getting into.

I didn't know day from night because I was not allowed to go outside. I cried out to God from that horrible place. *'Please God, take me out of here. I don't know if I can go on any longer. If I can't leave this place, then please just let me die. Dear God, I want to go home. Please let me go home. I can't do this anymore.'*

For me those dirty little rooms and those brutal and careless people were my entire world. They were the only people who I knew and saw in life. It was torture for me to stay there but I didn't know what would happen if I left. The traffickers told me it would get much worse. I knew almost nothing about the outside world, so I believed them.

Customers used to ask me why I stayed in the brothel and I said, "because my family is poor so I stay here to help my family". I was told to say that but it was also true.

Chapter 9

After about a year, I finally got some good news. I would be moving to Sonagachi where my aunt was living. The work was the same but I was happy because I thought that I would finally get the love of my aunt.

All the people working at the brothel in Sonagachi were from villages in Nepal or Manipur, an Indian state that borders Myanmar. I did enjoy my aunt's love and it was nice to be near her, but the brothel was controlled by Laxmi's aunt. My aunt, like me, was just working there. She had no power to help or protect me. Laxmi was not there with me in Sonagachi, despite it being her aunt's place.

In fact, Sonagachi was much worse for me than the brothel in Haldia, because there were more customers and they were more demanding and violent. We could only take a shower once or twice a week because of the lack of water.

The building was divided into four apartments with many tiny rooms. The rooms where we saw customers were subdivided by hanging sheets on clotheslines. There were two entrances to the brothel, which were always guarded, one at the front door, and one at the back. People were always watching those gates, and if you got too close to the gates, someone would immediately notice and send you back inside.

From 7:30 am to midnight each day, I had to stand in front of the building with the other girls. Even after midnight, I couldn't sleep because I had to serve late night customers. Each morning, they woke me up at 6:00 to get ready to be at the gate by 7:30am. We stood there the whole day. I don't know how we didn't collapse. Some older girls used to come and bring a banana with two or three pieces of *puri* (bread) and curry for me. I ate it standing up. I had to stand in line with the others until a customer came along and asked me to go with him.

In some ways, it was better to get a customer than to stand at the gate for hours with your legs aching. If you had a customer, you could rest just for a few seconds on the bed.

The madam used to tell me to stay inside the gate and never go out on the main road, because if the police found me, they would take me away, as I was still very small. At that time, I was thirteen years old. She told me the police would lock me up forever, and beat me, and I would never get to go home.

We survived by living moment to moment, and immediately forgetting whatever had just happened. In time, all my memories became jumbled. I couldn't hold any thought in my head for very long. I forgot what my life had been before. I forgot who I had once been.

Customers used to ask how much I wanted for one time, two times or the whole night. I was told to say 100 rupees ($1.50) for one time and 500 rupees ($8) for the whole night. The rooms where we took customers had five or six beds, with a curtain providing a small bit of privacy. There was also a big bed where the madams could sit and eat and watch TV while they watched over us. There were no toilets inside the building. There was only one toilet for the whole building, so some water was stored in a small bucket, and a small part of the room was set aside for us to wash our bodies after being with customers.

Whenever I had a customer, I used to try to rest for a few minutes on the bed before going back out, but Laxmi's aunt always noticed and made me go straight back outside. She scolded me if I didn't wear makeup, and she scolded me if I took too long to do my makeup.

Sometimes, in the late morning, I was allowed to nap for a few hours under a bed. They hid me because some women whom they used to call 'the contraceptive ladies' would come to check whether young girls were being kept in the brothel. If those ladies found small girls in the brothel, they would take the girls away with them. The bosses told us if those ladies took you away, you would never be seen again.

They told stories of girls cut up into pieces and left on the railway tracks, or locked in water barrels, or otherwise murdered. They had us convinced that our only chance of surviving and someday going home was to stay in the brothel and work hard, and to trust no one from outside, neither the police, nor the contraceptive ladies.

Each day was the same, and each day was a nightmare. Sometimes today I hear people saying things like 'the traffic was a nightmare,' or 'that class is a nightmare'. People say it lightly, so it has lost some of its meaning. But during that time in Sonagachi, I can truly say my nightmares came in the daytime. Nothing that my mind could dream up while sleeping was worse than the reality of every day in that place.

Most of the people who lived in that part of the red light area were from my village or district. Some of them are still there to this day. There were little girls, young women, and old ladies. There were married couples and young men who had grown up there, sons of the women in prostitution. Some men were the traffickers and pimps of their own sisters. One guy from my village prostituted his own sisters and beat them savagely.

Sometimes when a charity was coming to look for children in the brothel, the madam would hide me under the bed between boxes covered with blankets, or up on the rooftop, which could be very wet and cold.

One day, some people came into the brothel and found a young girl. I watched it all from my hiding place under my bed. They didn't seem like mean or dangerous people. Actually, they were talking very gently and comforting that girl, who was crying and shaking. For several minutes, I considered going to them and asking them to take me out too. My heart was pounding as I tried to get up the nerve to come out from under the bed. I came so close to doing it.

But in the end, I stayed where I was. I had been taught well by my traffickers, and by my life in the village, to trust no one.

A few weeks later, the managers found out that the police were coming to our building to look for young girls. They got this information from corrupt policemen who would come to the brothel to collect bribes, either in cash, or in free services from the girls.

The managers sent me out for the day with an older girl. They expected the police to come very early that day, at 6:00 am. So they sent us out at 5:00 am. The older girl took me to a place called Victoria Memorial. It was a large and very beautiful marble building, the grandest building I had ever seen. We walked all around the monument, took a horse ride, and bought some snacks from a vendor. We sat under a tree to eat the food. Sitting under that tree, for the first time in over a year, I enjoyed a little moment of peace. I was not afraid.

Unfortunately, it did not last long, because while we were eating, the police arrived in a Jeep. The older girl quickly told me what to say. She said, "Tell them that we only just met at the Victoria Memorial, that we don't know each other, that you are working in a beauty parlor and that you are twenty-one years old".

Then she took off quickly, leaving me there. The police came up and asked me my name, age, and what work I was doing. I told them all the lies that I had been instructed to tell, but when they asked me my address, I didn't know what to say. The older girl hadn't advised me on that. I had heard the name Sonagachi, so I said that I lived there. That got the police very suspicious because it is a well- known red light area and I was obviously not twenty-one years old. The police found the other girl and started questioning her, pointing at me. She walked away from the police, came towards me quickly and told me to run. We ran away and got into a taxi.

As the taxi drove away, we saw that the police car was right behind us. I began throwing up, because I was very anxious and still not used to riding in cars. The older girl told the driver to drive very fast. Then she got on her mobile phone and asked someone for money. We stopped on the way, and a lady handed us a stack of rupee notes. Then we drove to a place called Nico Park. It was a large park full of amusements and rides, and throngs of people. The police couldn't find us there, so we stayed the rest of the day there. It wasn't relaxing like Victoria, because by then I was terrified that the police would catch me and lock me up forever, or worse.

The older girl called the brothel to see if the police who were looking for minor girls had left. They told her that the police had indeed gone, so she took me back to Sonagachi. When I returned home. Laxmi's aunt scolded me harshly because I had told the police that I lived in Sonagachi and jeopardized her business. I didn't say anything because I was scared of her, and because my mother had taught me to never raise my voice to elders.

Maybe the fact that girls are raised this way is part of the problem. We are taught to be obedient, to take care of others, to put others first, especially the male members of our family. We are not taught to speak up for ourselves. We are raised to be the perfect prey, in a world full of predators.

Two months later, as I was brushing my teeth one morning, the madam grabbed me and shoved me under a bed. She piled some luggage in front of the bed and they covered me with blankets from all sides so that the police wouldn't recognize me as a human being. The police had come to the brothel with a picture of a small girl. They couldn't find that particular girl from their photo, so they pulled out another young girl, and arrested the brothel owner.

Due to repeated checking of the brothel by the police and anti-trafficking charities, I was sent back to the first brothel, in Haldia.

How was it that of all the people who came into my life, no one raised their voice? In the village, little children would sometimes put their hands into the fire because they don't know that it burns and kills. When adults see that situation, they immediately move the child away from the fire. They tell the child not to put her hand in the fire because it burns. In my life just the opposite happened. I didn't want to go near the fire, but the adults in my life said that it's good to go into the fire and it doesn't do any harm.

Chapter 10

Smita Singh grew up in Kolkata, but until she was thirty years old, she didn't even know where the Sonagachi red light area was. She had been working in the social sector for many years as a psychologist, but like many people, she believed that the women in red light areas wanted to be there. She thought they chose prostitution as a career because it was easy money. Later, she found out how false, and how damaging that belief was.

Smita spent much of her career working as a substance abuse counselor. By 2006, she was ready for a change. As she began searching for a new job, a colleague told her that an organization called IJM was coming to town, looking for an Aftercare Director. Smita sent in her resume and passed the first screening. But when she was invited to Mumbai for a second interview, her father was critically ill. She was very disappointed to lose the opportunity, but she couldn't leave her father as he was dying. Apparently, that job was not meant to be.

But then in October, IJM contacted Smita again. Her father had since passed away, so she went to the office, and had a chat with the Director. The next day, she was invited to fly to Mumbai for an interview, and by the end of that interview, she was hired.

Just a month after she joined the office, Smita worked her first rescue raid. It was completely different from anything she had done or seen in her previous job, or in fact in her entire life. The condition of the girls was appalling. The inhumanity of the traffickers was beyond anything she could ever have imagined. Smita had no clue how the raid was going to unfold. She was nervous about her role, which was to counsel the girls and convince them that they were not about to be taken out of the frying pan and into the fire.

On that raid, the team rescued four young girls from a brothel in Sonagachi red light area. The girls were from the *Agrawali* caste, a tribal group in India who had historically worked as entertainers. In olden times, the Agrawali were musicians and circus folk. In the modern era, as those traditions went out of fashion, they turned to trafficking and prostitution. They began routinely selling their daughters into brothels. Like the Tamang in Nepal, the Agrawali had normalized child prostitution. Selling girls and women was the main source of the community's income.

After the four Agrawali girls were rescued, and processed by the police and court, they were supposed to be brought before the Child Welfare Committee (CWC). The CWC is the state agency responsible for deciding where rescued girls are placed. At that time, survivors were almost always placed in a government-run shelter in the outskirts of the city.

Smita had heard some concerning stories about that particular shelter home. There had been some worrying reports of abuse, and even trafficking inside the home. The building seemed very enclosed, with razor wire all around its high gates. There was no good food, counseling or opportunities there. It was not a happy place for traumatized children.

Smita would not be allowed access, even though she had already formed a bond of trust with the girls.

She started crying and begging her team not to bring the girls to the CWC that day. She knew that if they did bring them, the girls would be sent immediately to the government home. But the girls had to be taken to the CWC, according to the law. Later that night, they were indeed assigned to the government shelter home.

Smita followed the police car that transported the girls, all the way across Kolkata for three miserable hours. She cried the entire way. When they finally arrived, she was not allowed past the iron entry gate.

"All I saw was this huge gate, and within it another tiny gate, which opened, and the girls were swallowed into the pitch darkness. I felt so helpless," said Smita.

Thankfully, another local agency, Sanlaap, was working at the government home. They agreed to sneak Smita in as one of their staff, so she got to see the girls she had helped to rescue from time to time. Through this experience, Smita became very determined to find more compassionate shelter homes for rescued girls.

A few months after Smita began working at IJM, Don Gerred came from America to lead the office's legal efforts. Smita and Don quickly became good friends. They were both practical types, not given to emotional displays. They were quietly, doggedly committed. Smita appreciated Don's quirky humor. She was not intimidated by him, unlike some of the others in the office. Smita was not intimidated by anyone.

The rescue raids got more frequent and more successful when Don took over as Director of the office. But in the summer of 2008, Smita began feeling burned out and exhausted. She badly injured her leg, and didn't think she would be physically able to go on brothel raids anymore. Emotionally, she had been worn down by the pain of seeing girls in such terrible circumstances. She had been heartbroken many times when she helped to rescue girls, only to see them put into homes that were not good for them. They often ran away, back to the red light areas. The brothels were an evil they at least were familiar with. Their friends and family members were there. They saw no other alternatives for their future.

In the last year, thirty-two girls who Smita helped to free from brothels had been lost. They didn't get enough support to overcome the trauma, stigma and other huge obstacles they faced. She felt frustrated, and even a little hopeless. What was the point in rescuing girls if you can't give them a good life? One rescued girl was placed in a government home, and seemed to be doing so well, but then she ran away. She was trafficked by another girl at the shelter, who took her to a brothel in Mumbai.

Smita decided it was time for her to stop doing anti-trafficking work. Not only was she discouraged, but she had begun to feel that the work she was doing was not effective. It was not leading to long-term, positive life changes for survivors. So she applied for, and got a job at another agency.

"I had never heard God speak to me in dreams, or anything like that," said Smita. "Frankly I had always been skeptical of that kind of thing. But this one time, I had a very strange and powerful dream. I dreamed of a friend asking me to read a passage from the Bible: Joshua 6:22. I woke up and told my mum about the dream. My mum said 'Well, go read it and see what it says.' I refused. As a psychologist, I don't believe in getting signs and numbers from dreams. I watched some TV instead. Scrolling through channels, I came across a guy giving a sermon, and his name was Joshua Daniel. That struck me again, but still I did not open a Bible. The voiceover on the TV sermon sounded just like one of my colleagues from IJM. So I called him to ask if he had been doing voiceover work, and indeed he had. Finally my mom prevailed upon me and I opened the Bible to find out what the passage said. It read, 'Go into the prostitute's house and bring her out and all who belong to her, because you have promised'".

Smita was moved by that experience. It convinced her that she needed to stay on at her job. Perhaps there was still a promise for her to fulfill, on behalf of girls in forced prostitution. It was too soon to give up.

Finding suitable homes where survivors could heal and rebuild their lives was a hard, but hugely important battle for Smita. Few homes in Kolkata provided the opportunities that she knew survivors needed. A seed was planted in her, to someday create a home that could address trauma, give hope, and prepare survivors to be independent. But that dream would take time to bring to life. Smita needed safe shelter immediately for the girls she was helping to rescue.

Sanlaap, (the organization that had helped Smita to sneak into the government shelter posing as one of their staff), had their own shelter home in Kolkata. Smita visited and found it to be a pleasant place, run by a caring staff. She built a strong partnership with Sanlaap. Once that partnership was in place, she could advocate for girls to be placed at

Sanlaap Home. The girls would be in a safe and nurturing environment, and she and her team would be allowed to visit as often as they liked.

Chapter 11

I was back at the old brothel in Haldia, and everything was exactly as awful as before. The customers came continually and the managers would call us down to the hotel bar, and scold or punish us if their commands were not followed. The house owner would visit occasionally to check on things and collect his share of the earnings. We were never allowed outside.

Compared to my village, Haldia was a huge city, but compared to Kolkata, it was more like a small town. It was a port city, and many trucks came through to pick up or drop off goods at the port. There was a major highway in front of the hotel, and truck drivers made up a large percentage of the customers.

In Haldia as in Sonagachi, the police sometimes came, looking for children in the brothel. The house owner had another building, which had just been constructed. Sometimes we would hide from the police there, up on the roof. Every night a police Jeep used to come stop at the gate of the hotel. The manager would give some money to the policemen, and they would go on their way. Every single night, those policemen made the choice to ignore the suffering of children for a few rupees.

I developed some bad habits to keep myself going. I started to smoke and drink. I was destroying myself, day by day. No money was given to me from the managers, but occasionally I would get tips from the customers. I bought snacks, alcohol and cigarettes with that money.

I tried to quit drinking and smoking, but things got so bad, and I became so hopeless that I couldn't stop myself. I felt like I was not a human being. I felt like an animal in the forest, constantly on guard, never able to rest. I was thirteen years old and had lived seventeen months in the red light area. I was tired of people and the world. I stopped praying to go home and started wishing I could just die.

Then, one night in September, everything changed.

In the evening, two customers came who had never been to the hotel before. They seemed richer than our usual clientele. When the greedy managers saw the potential for bigger earnings, they came up to the bedrooms to call all the girls down. Everyone came downstairs except a few girls who were already busy with customers. There were about twenty girls standing in front of the two new customers, but they said that they didn't like anyone.

We all sat down, but after a few seconds, many cars pulled up outside the hotel. Suddenly, some ladies and a large number of police officers entered the hotel. The two customers were undercover operatives. They had come with the rescue organization IJM to raid the brothel and rescue us.

One lady was running around like crazy, waving a giant flashlight. She was barely over five feet tall, with a slightly round, not athletic physique, but she looked like a fierce and powerful warrior. She was on fire with righteous anger and the urge to protect us, the desire for justice. One minute she was yelling at the traffickers, trying to stop them from running away. The next minute she was talking gently to us girls, promising us we would be safe, taking us by the hands and pulling us out of that place, gently but with a kind of power and urgency. That lady, I later learned, was Smita.

At one point, Smita waved her giant flashlight in a brothel manager's face, shouting, "Don't you dare try to run away, or I will hit you on the head with this!"

Don and his team had worked for months setting up this rescue. It was because of their careful planning and strategy that the raid was so successful. Through the undercover work of the operatives, the IJM team knew there were Nepali minor girls at the brothel, but they thought there were only three or four of us. One of the girls in the brothel, Ashayana, was only ten years old. She had been the focal point of the case.

There had been many hurdles, traffic jams, and things not working out before the raid finally succeeded. Again and again, the raid kept getting delayed or called off. Finally, on September 3rd, 2008, everything seemed to be in place. The team assembled at a police station in central Kolkata. They were crushed when they found out that they couldn't do the raid because Haldia was outside the territory of the Kolkata police. They were told to try again with the district police for Haldia. They would have to wait a whole day to do so, and they lost all hope of rescuing Ashayana. Someone was sure to warn the traffickers by then.

The next day, Smita, along with IJM's lawyer Eliza, and a case worker named Rupa accompanied the Haldia district police to conduct the raid.

Vic, the Lead Investigator, also came along but he had to stay in the car because he was white and would have drawn too much attention. Don was not there for the same reason. He was in Nepal following the progress of the raid by cell phone.

Just before the raid, the team went to the police headquarters in Haldia to meet with the District Head of Police. This was necessary because there was a huge problem with corruption. Many raids had failed because someone inside the police department leaked information to the traffickers.

When the team arrived at the police station, all of the people who were going to go on the raid were called into the captain's office, and immediately told to hand over their cell phones, to prevent anyone tipping off the traffickers. The captain was going to lead the raid himself - undercover. He was very committed and enthusiastic. He was dressed very nicely, so he changed into simpler clothes, but his shoes were still very fancy which would have given him away. So, the IJM driver Tapan loaned him his shoes.

The plan was to drop everyone ten minutes from the brothel, and have people walk there in groups of two. The brothel was on a lonely stretch of road, just off a highway, with a lot of trucks parked outside. The police surrounded the building and some entered from the back, some from the front.

Smita, Eliza and Rupa entered from the front. They had studied the undercover footage so they knew where the girls would be sitting, at the back of the hotel bar. Sure enough, four of five girls were sitting in that area on a bench. Hanging above their heads were the little bags containing notebooks where the managers would track their customers.

Smita got those five girls on the bench out. A large crowd began to gather outside, to see what all the fuss was about. Sometimes the crowd becomes raucous or violent when there is a raid, but thankfully that didn't happen this time. The owner wasn't there, but several managers were arrested.

Smita, Eliza and Rupa searched the brothel and kept finding more and more girls, including me. Girls kept coming out of the rooms with customers. The customers ran away as fast as they could.

Often when there is a rescue raid, the girls are hidden, behind walls or in tiny compartments. But in this case, the traffickers had no idea the raid was coming, so it was business as usual. All the girls were out in the open.

"The police gave us fifteen minutes and said we could take out any girls we found," said Smita.
"It was like a crazy sale at a store, all these lovely kids. We were pulling them out without counting. The most shocking thing for me was seeing how young they were". At fourteen, I was among the older girls. Ashayana was only ten, and tiny.

As the women of IJM kept running out the building with more girls, Vic, hiding in the back of the van, kept asking, "How many did we get?"

"We've got five, now we've got ten... no wait it's twelve.... no, fourteen!" Smita answered.

They put all the girls into their cars, to take us to the police station. The police tried to catch all the managers and madams, but several escaped. Of the five managers, two were arrested that day.

Out of thirty girls, nineteen were freed from slavery that day, and I was one of them. It was, in many ways, the beginning of my life.

Chapter 12

Nineteen of us had been pulled out of the brothel and squeezed into IJM's two cars, but the battle was far from over. Next, we needed to be taken to the police station for processing, a situation the IJM team had faced many times before. There were some very corrupt people working there.

Smita worried that it would be a challenge to manage so many girls in such a risky environment. She and the other IJM ladies stayed with us throughout the night. The large party of girls and IJM staff took over one room of the police station. They removed the furniture and put down blankets so we could rest.

As soon as we were settled, Smita and her team began to gather information: names, ages, and where we came from. Everyone claimed to be nineteen or twenty, even the littlest girls. Eventually they discovered that three of the nineteen girls were over eighteen. The rest were between ten and fifteen.

We had been taught to give false names and addresses, so that is mostly what we did. I told them the correct name of my village but everything else I told them - my name and what happened to me - was false. I must admit I was one of the least cooperative. Some girls, like me, were angry and argumentative. Others, like little Ashayana, were withdrawn and not willing or able to talk at all. Some girls had literally just been pulled out of a session with a customer and were half-dressed and disoriented. Every single one of us had been brainwashed by our traffickers to believe that our only hope was to keep working in the brothel and to keep our mouths shut.

One by one, girls were taken to the next room to be questioned by the police. Smita and Eliza, IJM's lawyer, came with us. I refused to cooperate at all. I didn't know why I should trust the rescuers or the police. Policemen came to the brothel every night to collect bribes, or to have sex with girls instead of a cash bribe. Most of us didn't share any information that night. But all the lawyer needed to know was that we were not from Kolkata, that we were working in a brothel, and that we were underage.

Smita guessed girls' ages based on their appearance and wrote that down on the papers. The IJM team had to do all the paperwork because this was a District Police station, so they did everything by hand. They had no computers or printers. Whenever the IJM did a raid with the police, they had to bring our own portable computers and printers.

"Even on that first night, a few girls stood out as having innate leadership skills," said Smita. "They were very vocal about controlling the others".

I was one of the bossy ones, telling the other girls what they should say or not say, and how they should behave.

All night long, Smita talked to girls, accompanied girls for questioning, and filled out paperwork. When she wasn't talking or writing, she was praying silently for the lost, wounded children sprawled out on the floor in every corner of the room. Adrenaline was still coursing through her veins from the raid, and that helped her to stay awake through the long night.

At one point, Smita asked me why I worked in the brothel. "My family are poor and I need to help them!" I shouted back at her. "If my family were rich like yours, then maybe I could study and get a better job. I have no education and no skills, and my family is very poor, and I am a girl, so who will provide a good job for me?"

She spoke softly back to me. She said that she would help me. Something like hope came inside me and I closed my mouth.

We stayed all night in the police station. The ladies gave us food, and little packages containing a toothbrush, a bar of soap, a comb, a towel and a night dress. There was only one package to share between every two girls, because they hadn't expected to rescue so many of us. I washed my face but didn't brush my teeth because I didn't care to share a toothbrush. No one tried to force me. This was a very small boundary, but it was the first one I had been able to set for myself in more than two years.

In the morning, the police took some pictures of us standing in front of a wall. Then they sent us to sit in a big police van. I was pretty sure they would drive us back to the brothel then. I only felt a little disappointed. I hadn't really expected to remain free for long.

But then, instead of driving back to the brothel, the police van took us somewhere which they called 'Court'. That day IJM did not have their cars, so we had to ride in a police bus, with bars on the window. That was quite humiliating. We felt like we were prisoners. We were vomiting a lot. There were no windows, so we had to vomit on the floor. Because it looked like a prison bus, people were staring at us like we were criminals.

When we arrived at the court, for just a few minutes we were put in a small jail cell. Smita and the other ladies argued forcefully with the guards that we shouldn't be locked in a cell. We were not criminals, we were trafficked children.

They got us out of the jail cell and into a small room at the back of the courthouse. There we waited for an hour, and everyone got anxious and irritable. We had been up all night. Our lives were hanging in the balance.

Smita explained that we were waiting to get orders for placement in a shelter home. A few hours later, one of the IJM ladies came to tell us that sixteen of us were going to a home called Sanlaap. Three of our friends had to be separated from the group and sent to another shelter because they were over eighteen. One of those three was an aunt of mine.

Sixteen of us got into one van, and those three girls got into another car. That was a very sad moment for me, watching those three sisters driven off in one direction, while we were driven in another. I had no idea where we were going, and scant hopes that it would be somewhere good.

It was all too much to process - the raid, the long night at the station, the police bus, the jail cell, the hours of questioning, the separation from three of our friends. I had just lived through seventeen months of fear and violence, and now I was being taken somewhere else, outside of my control. I closed my eyes and shut everything out. It looked like sleeping but it was deeper than that. It was something I learned to do in the brothel. I made myself not there at all.

Chapter 13

Several hours later, we pulled up to the Sanlaap shelter. I was surprised by the size and scope of the place. I had never seen anything like it before. There was a large iron gate surrounding the complex. Inside there were two big buildings - the dormitories and a dining hall - and three small buildings - an office, infirmary and vocational training center. In front of the gate, there was a big pond. The complex was lush with flowers and shade trees. There was a little bamboo cottage where they gave counseling and schooling.

The shelter home staff welcomed us. They took us into the girls' dorm and gave us food and clean clothes to wear. Unfortunately, the clothes were the same for all of us. They were green and yellow loose trousers and tunics, a hideous color combination! We thought they looked like prison uniforms. That seemed fitting because at that point, I was convinced we were either in jail or in some different kind of brothel. I felt terribly uneasy.

They showed us our beds, which were surprisingly nice. We each had our own bed, covered in printed sheets in many different colors and designs. The sheets were so clean! We ate dinner and went to bed. We had not slept at all the night before, and despite my anxiety, I soon fell deeply asleep.

The next morning, Indrani Sinha, the founder of Sanlaap, came to meet us. Indrani was a force of nature, no-nonsense and strict with her staff, but incredibly loving and gentle to the girls. She was a roundish woman with short hair and thick black glasses. She wore simple practical clothes and shoes, despite being a high class person. Energy seemed to flow out of her in waves, and everyone was drawn to it.

Indrani had worked to combat violence against women and girls for more than twenty years. She was one of India's most respected anti-trafficking activists. She began her career as an English teacher at a posh school, but soon realized that her passion lay elsewhere. She wanted to work with the most vulnerable women and girls.

Indrani started Sanlaap (which means dialogue) in 1987 after spending time in the red light areas doing a research project. The women and girls there told her about the powerlessness they felt living in prostitution. They shared stories like mine, about being tricked by family members or neighbors, with false promises and with no idea what kind of work they would be forced to do.

Women told her that they continued to work in brothels even after they were older and no longer locked in, because they had no other means to support themselves. Most of them also had young children to support. Indrani had to do something to help these women and girls. She started with small projects, and over time opened the shelter, and many drop-in centers in the red light areas. Sanlaap also did a lot of work to educate the society about girl trafficking.

Not everyone agreed with Indrani's approach, because there was (and still is) a movement to legalise prostitution in India. This movement is based on the idea that sex workers will be more empowered and safer if prostitution is legal. Some people from the sex workers' rights movement deny that sex trafficking and child trafficking are a problem in India. Indrani fought strongly against this way of thinking.

"Before we speak on the issue of legalization of prostitution," she wrote, "we need to recognize prostitution for what it is: a situation that begins with rape and a choiceless choice and continues with denial and exploitation. As women and as activists, it is our responsibility to create the options and the spaces which would prevent the birth of this violence...Would we advocate that child labor be legalized just because it exists? A form of violence cannot be accepted merely because it is there and has been for centuries. The basis of its existence needs to be challenged."

Indrani and Sanlaap also took in girls with HIV and AIDS. Other shelters would not accept such girls, and they were not welcome in their villages, so they had nowhere to go if they were rescued. There were several HIV positive girls at Sanlaap when we arrived.

The first few days at Sanlaap were hard. The clothes they had given us were not only ugly, they were scratchy and uncomfortable. The iron gates felt strange and frightening to us. The home felt not like a simple house, but more like a prison, with a huge iron gate that looked like bars. I was convinced we were not safe, and would soon be sent back to the brothel, or into an even worse brothel, or that men would come to Sanlaap to abuse us. I was waiting for one of these things to happen, steeling myself to cope with what was surely coming next.

It was difficult to communicate with the other girls and the staff. We didn't speak much Bengali. In the brothel, we were just taught a little Hindi, so we could communicate with customers from different parts of India. One of the Sanlaap staff knew just a few words of Nepali, and of course no one spoke Tamang. IJM had Nepali staff, but they only came once or twice a week.

Besides the language barrier, there was an emotional barrier to communicating. We had no idea how to express ourselves. It took months to find the words for what we wanted to say.

A few days after we arrived at Sanlaap, Don Gerred came to visit, bringing his little girls, who were seven and eight years old. They looked more like dolls than human beings to me, because of their fair, fair skin and yellow hair. We were all still so traumatized at that point, quite fearful and uncomfortable with anyone outside our little Tamang circle. Don's daughters somehow knew just how to be with us. They had a mobile phone and they showed us how to take pictures of them, and then they took pictures of us. Very gently and shyly, they crept in among us so we could all look at the little screen together. They were even smaller than the smallest of us, so it felt safe. Don himself kept a respectful distance. He sat down as soon as he arrived and made himself as small and non-threatening as possible.

A few days after that, Smita and the other IJM counselors came to see us again. One of the counselors, Rupa, was Nepali, while the others were from different parts of India. Again, they asked us for our addresses and other background information. They needed to know what had happened, in order to begin building the court case, but we still did not trust them. I didn't want to talk about what had happened over the last seventeen months to anyone, let alone a stranger. Some girls told them the truth, while others (like me) kept giving them false information and speaking rudely to them.

They responded calmly to our angry outbursts. They gently pointed out that while they were Nepali citizens with permission to come to India, we were illegal aliens. We had no citizenship and no right nor reason to remain in India.

"You are not vegetables to be sold in the market!" Smita told us, that day and many times after. "You are worth more than that. You have human rights".

The first time we had to appear in court, they hired a big bus to take us there. It was about a week after we came to the shelter. It took three hours to drive to the district court, so they stopped to get us some food halfway. But nobody was getting off that bus. Some girls started crying, some grew rigid and withdrew into themselves.

Smita said "It's going to be a long day. You guys should eat". Every single girl refused. We stayed in our seats, and nobody said a word. Finally, the youngest girl, Ashayana, asked the question that all of us were thinking.

"Is this where you are going to sell us again?"

We were very anxious because the bus had stopped at a hotel restaurant on the highway. It looked very similar to the brothel where we had been kept.

Over several months, the counselors helped me to understand the truth of the situation. They explained over and over that we had been trafficked, that we had done nothing wrong. What was done to *us* was wrong. At first, we didn't believe them. We would shout at them, begging them to get us out of the shelter and back to the brothel. We believed that that was the only way we could ever get home to Nepal, because that was what the traffickers had told us. We were brainwashed to believe that our abusers were our only hope, and that prostitution was our only option.

We had been raised to believe that it was our responsibility to help support our families by any means necessary. We were raised to be obedient and agreeable, to believe that we were not important. We were taught from an early age to put our needs last. Everything in our society was designed around the needs and desires of men and boys. The traffickers played on these beliefs, to keep us from running away or fighting back.

Over the weeks and months, the counselors taught us many things. They taught us about human rights, about the laws against child trafficking. They taught me to believe in myself. They promised that if I wanted to go home, they would help me.

There came a time when I and eight of my friends finally decided to trust them. We stopped asking to go back to the brothel and we began working with the IJM team on the legal case. Later the other girls rescued with us also stopped asking to go back, except for one girl. She was never able to believe there was another way. She escaped from the shelter one night and ran back to the red light area. I understand why she ran away. Her spirit had been broken, and she saw no other way for her life.

I, on the other hand, was seeing all kinds of new opportunities for my life, things I had never before imagined. Slowly I began to trust the Sanlaap and the IJM staff, to like them and then to love them. These wonderful people helped me in so many ways. I started to see the world, and myself differently. Gradually, everyone began to dream.

Chapter 14

When she first started counseling us, IJM counselor Rupa Chetri didn't have a lot of expertise in counseling trafficking survivors. She had studied psychology in college, but had little real-world experience. Rupa was a twenty-eight- year- old Nepali woman. She was slim with delicate features, and a gentle tone of voice.

At first, Rupa had no idea how to do things the standard way, so she had to use her imagination. Learning alongside us day by day, she and the other counselors came up with their own counseling techniques.

Trafficked people have unique psychological challenges. Those who were sold at an early age have experienced chronic stress. Trauma has taken place repeatedly in their lives, beginning on the day when they trusted somebody and then were sold into a brothel. Again, they trusted somebody, and then they were again sold to another place, and then another. Instead of experiencing a limited period of stress, they have been under continuous, long-term stress. Even the rescue can be a traumatic experience. Girls aren't expecting to be rescued, and again they are taken from whatever safety they have created for themselves.

So the first thing survivors need is to feel safe. The counselors spent a lot of time creating a safe space for our sessions, allowing us to set boundaries, making sure we were physically comfortable, assuring us again and again that we were safe.

When you are in a brothel, you forget who you are. You are probably not called by your real name. You have to wear a mask at all times. You can never relax, because you might be called down to service a customer at any moment of the night or day. You could be under attack at any moment.

The stress is unbearable, so to cope with it, girls go into fight-flight-freeze mode. Many times at the brothel, girls would play dead when they were with a customer. They were beyond fight or flight. They didn't even seem to realize what was happening to their bodies. Their brains would just completely shut down. They might use alcohol or drugs to help them shut down, which is what I started doing towards the end. I wanted to shut down, and I also wanted to destroy myself.

When the raid happened, the rescuers were strangers to us. Our alarm systems were activated again. Now different people were taking us, and everything was again outside of our control. It was a trigger for many girls, being forcibly taken from whatever safe zone they had been able to create for themselves. The rescuers used the same kind of words as the traffickers, and we couldn't tell the difference. When they took us to the police station, that was another trigger. Some girls had been used or abused by policemen, or they went to the police for help and were refused. Everyone had seen the police come by in their Jeep each evening to collect their bribes.

Most of the girls' stories were fragmented. They couldn't remember everything in the order it happened. Healing this kind of trauma is not a short process. It takes years. In order to heal, you have to bring all of those fragments together. You need to know and understand your own story. You have to remember who you are, both the literal details of your background and also who you are deep down inside. You have to learn to identify feelings and to reconnect your mind with your body. This was the hard, beautiful, necessary work we did for eighteen months with Rupa and the other counselors.

With their help, we approached these problems, and our healing, from many directions, through talk therapy, through meditation and relaxation exercises, through games and stories, through painting and dancing, through sisterhood, solidarity and love. Because Rupa had little formal counseling experience, she relied on her intuition and got more training as she went along. She went back to school in the evenings to get training in Cognitive Behavioral Therapy.

There were three counselors from IJM that worked with us and each had her own healing power. Rupa would come up with stories and metaphors to help us change the negative stories we were telling ourselves. Trishna was good at coming up with themes and prompts for our group talks. Swapnil was creative in the arts and designed workshops to help us work through issues without having to use words. Many of the problems and memories were difficult or embarrassing to talk about. Some of the younger girls didn't even know the words to describe what had happened to them.

Pain that comes through your body can't just be talked out. It also has to be released through physical activities. The art projects were helpful for that, as well as the dance and karate classes that Sanlaap offered.

One of Rupa's favorite metaphors was about a well. "Have you seen a well?" she asked. "How does a well look? It is deep and dark. What is in a well? Water. You pull it out with a bucket which is difficult. The water that comes out of a well is full of leaves and grit. Would you throw out the water?"

"No," we answered. "We would strain the water, removing the leaves and dirt. Then we would take it home and use it for cooking and washing dishes".

"The well represents the brothel, which is very dark and deep," Rupa told us. "We don't even know if we will be able to pull out the water from such a deep, dark well. The water is you girls. The bucket is us and the pulley is God. You have been hurt, but you are very precious. You are not something dirty and useless, to be thrown away. We are here to restore the water, together, and bring it home, to bless everyone".

Survivors rarely want to talk about their trauma. They don't want to remember what has happened to them. They have forgotten their feelings, and they have difficulty naming and recognizing feelings.

Rupa and the team came up with games that enabled us to share our feelings and gradually to talk about our experiences. In one of the games, they showed us pictures of people's faces, and we had to guess what the person was feeling from the expression on her face. At first we were terrible at it. We couldn't tell the difference from mildly irritated to totally enraged. But we were always happy to play any game, because we had lost so much of our childhoods.

When the counselors brought up the subject of family, at least one girl would always get up and walk away. No one wanted to think about her family. For most of us, our families were involved in trafficking us. They allowed it to happen, or they encouraged it. Some parents even trafficked their own children. I still don't understand how someone could do such a thing to their own child.

Very slowly, through the stories, games and art projects, the counselors led each girl back to her trafficking story. It was important that everyone find a way to talk about what happened.
At some point, you have to say it out loud to at least one person.

"Through play therapy, slowly we would build the girls' self-esteem, and teach them that the abuse was not their fault," said Rupa. "The first thing we learned was not to use dominating language. In Nepali, we have several different forms for the word 'you'. 'Timi' is the more casual way. We use it for close friends and family, but also for children, servants, people in lower positions or menial jobs. With the girls, we needed to speak with respect, and let them choose how they wanted to be addressed, whether formally or informally. The first mistake people make is to assert power. You can't force or rush survivors into telling their stories. Instead, you need to put the power back in their hands".

Every girl's healing journey was different. Some responded quickly and some took years to open up. I was somewhere in the middle.

We could always go to the counselors after group therapy and say, "I want to talk to you alone". We could choose whichever of the three counselors we felt most comfortable with. I did this many times. The counselors would always tell us, "If we say something that bothers you, you are free to get up and leave, or you can talk to one of us privately". I loved that they gave us that freedom, and that respect.

The main social issues survivors face are trust issues, PTSD, intrusive thoughts and memories, and Stockholm syndrome, where girls become bonded with the people who enslave them as a way to survive. Some girls even fall in love with their traffickers or clients and marry them.

There were a few girls living at Sanlaap who were not able to see beyond their abuse. They got stuck in their trauma, in their resentment and rage. That caused problems in their relationships with everyone at the shelter, other girls as well as the shelter staff.

Most survivors, while they were being exploited, had to fight for everything, whether it was their food, the number or type of clients they had to take, a space to sleep, or money. Constant struggle and competition became an ingrained pattern. They started to believe that if they were not aggressive, they wouldn't get their needs met.

Thankfully, other than the one Tamang girl who ran away, none of the girls in my group got stuck in their past, or in aggressive behavior patterns. I think this was largely because of the counseling we got from Rupa and the other counselors. They tried to discover what skills each girl had, no matter how small, so they could become her cheerleaders.

The counselors used games to gather information for our legal cases in a non-threatening way. In one of the games, everyone sat in a circle, and one of the counselors would say "Stand up if you like watermelon," or "Stand up if your favorite color is blue". Everyone who liked watermelon or the color blue would stand, and then we would exchange places in the circle with another girl who was also standing.

Next they would ask something slightly more personal, like "Stand up if you have a sister", or "Stand up if you come from such and such village". These games helped us to remember things about ourselves, and to learn things about each other. The questions also required us to look inside yourself and think about our own likes and dislikes. *Do* I like watermelon? What *is* my favorite color? At first, I honestly didn't know.

We had no choices in the brothel, about anything. We lost the ability to choose, to say out loud what we liked, what we wanted, or didn't want. We did every single thing according to the will and the desires of others.

One day we played a game where you put something salty or sour in your mouth to see how long you could hold it there, and what kind of face you would make. That game made us laugh so hard! It was designed to show us that our physical reactions are natural and normal. The game also helped us to connect our expressions and reactions to what we were feeling inside, a connection that had been broken when we were in the brothel.

When you put some honey in your mouth, replacing a nasty taste with a nice taste, your facial expression becomes happy. You have recovered from the bad thing. This was a way of demonstrating that it is possible to heal. Good experiences can take away the bad taste of negative experiences.

Sometimes Rupa brought props, like a boiled egg or a coconut. "You have to break the shell to bring out the goodness inside," she said. "You can't go through life with a hard shell and be your best self. There is still softness in you. The coconut looks hard from the outside. You guys look hard from the outside, too. So many people have hurt you, so you have built layer upon layer of shell to protect yourself. You don't want to talk to anyone, trust anyone, love anyone. It's normal, it's okay. But you have to allow, by your own choice, when you are ready, for the shell to crack. You have to make yourself vulnerable. When you do that, all the strength and beauty within you can come out. Yes, it will hurt to talk about these things, but only then can your true self come out".

The counselors asked us, "Do you want to be called by the name given you in the brothel, or by your village name? Do you want to be addressed with a familiar or a formal pronoun?"

They always made us say out loud what we preferred. The first time they asked me that, I felt strangely angry. It was a polite and considerate question. But I felt full of rage and had to leave the circle.

That was a few months after I came to Sanlaap. That day I started crying for the first time. I cried for such a long time. I couldn't stop crying and I was afraid I would never be able to stop. My sisters came around me and put their arms around me and held me for a long time while I wept and wept. And eventually I did stop crying and felt a little lighter. I feel like my healing began that day.

Sometimes we did mindfulness meditation, where we would lie down and try to feel every part of our bodies, from head to toe. They called it 'taking the score'. At first it was hard to concentrate on how my feet felt, or especially how my hips or stomach felt. I had disconnected from those parts of my body to survive. Slowly I became able to feel every part of myself, to love and honor every part of my body.

We talked about hormonal changes, sexual desire, how it is normal and healthy, and not a shameful thing. We learned that we can take control when we feel a natural attraction to the opposite sex. We learned about sexually transmitted diseases which you can get in a brothel. I had never heard of those before.

Many of us were so young when we were trafficked, we knew next to nothing about our bodies. Six months after we came to Sanlaap, one of the girls from our group had a baby. None of us even knew she was pregnant, and then one night, she began complaining about a terrible stomachache. She was taken to the hospital and the doctor said, "She's having her baby". It was such a shock. She didn't look pregnant at all. Many of us had irregular periods, and everyone had gained some healthy weight since we came to Sanlaap. Even if there were some clues, the girl might have been in denial about it.

One of the art projects was to draw our family tree. When the counselors explained the assignment, the girls who had traffickers in their family hung their heads in shame. They refused to do the project. It was especially complicated when one girls' family member was involved in the trafficking of another girl in the group. Sadly, this was the case for several of the Tamang girls. The counselors told us, that day and many times after, that it wasn't our fault if a family member was a trafficker. We didn't need to feel ashamed for the wrongdoings of others. We only needed to be responsible for our own actions.

This was a completely new concept for us, because in our culture, everyone is held accountable for the actions of their family members. We Nepalis are big on shame.

Sometimes when there had been a home study back in the village, the counselors would bring photos of a girl's sisters. Often, seeing those photos of their little sisters would motivate girls to share information which could protect their sisters. There was an ongoing need to gather information for our legal cases, to get traffickers prosecuted and ultimately to get us home to Nepal. But it was equally important to provide high quality counseling and to respect the privacy of individual girls. Sometimes this created a conflict for Rupa and the other counselors.

"In order to get a prosecution, we needed to find out who trafficked them, from where and how did they travel to India, where they were taken to, what were the connections between them," said Rupa. "They were young kids, twelve and thirteen years old, and they had been so badly hurt. Their well-being was the most important thing, more important than the case. We had to hunt for clues to build the case, slowly and so, so gently".

We were *freed* the night of the raid. But in many ways we were still not entirely free. Emotionally and spiritually, we were still locked in our own woundedness, self-blame, and trauma. We were still in fight, flight or freeze mode.

When I was first rescued, I truly had no idea that I had even been enslaved. I thought I was just fulfilling a responsibility to my family. I was just doing what almost every girl from my village did. I had no concept of the wrongness and violence of the situation. I thought I was the one who was wrong.

Until we accepted the painful reality that we *had* been enslaved, we could not fully embrace the gift of freedom. Until we experienced some emotional healing, we would keep torturing ourselves, as much as the traffickers tortured us, but in our own minds. Only when we remembered who we were, and found a way to give voice to what had happened to us, could our healing begin.

For twenty months, those healers used all their ingenuity and love to teach us how to be truly and completely free.

Chapter 15

In the early days at Sanlaap, I felt like a little child, growing and learning the systems of the world for the first time. I saw the possibility of a different life than I had ever imagined, beyond the brothels, beyond working in the fields and constantly struggling to survive. I began to imagine a future where my contribution would not be to earn money to help my family, but to change the village and to show a different way to the next generation. It was like a seed was planted and growing within me with a new hope. My life was beginning all over again.

I began to nurture a dream, to go back to my village and tell people the truth, that in India girls are forced to sell their bodies. When we go to India, we can get terrible diseases which will kill us. We are made to stand at a gate day and night, calling for customers. Small girls are given drugs to make them grow bigger and more developed. We are hungry, hurt and humiliated, day in and day out. The traffickers tell us that we will get to wear new clothes every day, but the reality is that we have nothing to call our own, and we have no choice about what clothes we wear or anything else. We cannot keep the money which we earn by selling our bodies. We are made to sleep with all different types of men. We are not seen as human beings.

I yearned to tell all these things to my family, to the villagers, and especially to the young girls in my village. I wanted to share with them the sorrows that I experienced in India. I decided then that going back to my village, and telling the truth about what happened to me, was the only way to stop other girls from having to live it.

Smita and the others always told us that they would help us get back home. They thought they would be able to get us back in a few months, but actually it ended up taking nearly two years, because the courts kept delaying and changing the court dates. The Indian legal system is very bureaucratic, and it took a long time to work our way through it.

During the long wait, we got involved in things at the shelter. I began to wake up and remember who I really was. I started studying in an informal school inside the shelter. When I first came to Sanlaap, I didn't know how to read. I only knew a few letters. I remembered nothing of what that man taught me in those nine months in the house, before going to the brothel in Haldia. After seventeen months in the brothel, I forgot everything. All the things that happened kind of erased my memory for a while.

So at Sanlaap, I had to start over from the beginning. I was almost fully grown, and I had seen and experienced the absolute worst of life. It felt strange to be singing 'A is for Apple'. But at the same time it felt good, to be a kid again.

At the Sanlaap informal school, there was one lady teacher, Chanda, who taught all the subjects. There was also a male teacher, who we called Grandfather. He came to teach the ninth and tenth grade girls, but he included us in his teaching as well. We were the same age as the ninth-graders but we were doing kindergarten work at first.

Grandfather saw something in me, and he wanted to encourage it. He and his wife used to tutor me in math. I studied all day, every day. I learned a lot of English from all of the teachers. I loved to read, and Chanda would give me books. I had never before had so many adults caring about me and trying to help me. It was incredible to me that they didn't want anything from me in return. Their kindness was pure.

After a while, I took on three or four students of my own. These were my friends who had never gone to school and were struggling. Teaching them made me learn faster as well. Outside of my close circle of Tamang sisters, I also became friends with other girls at the home, like Leeza, who had been rescued at age nine from a brothel run by her own mother. She had been at the shelter since she was little. Leeza was very smart, and advanced in her education. I aspired to be like her.

Once I had learned to read, I read a book about sexual abuse and violence. That was when I realized for the first time that I had been sexually abused in my childhood. I understood then that what happened with my two male relatives in the village was not normal or right, and that it wasn't my fault. That was such a relief. It had been a heavy burden.

I joined a youth leadership program. The youth leadership group used to publish magazines, and I had three short stories published in our magazine. I was so proud! That was the first time in my life that something I did was recognized and celebrated. One of my stories was called 'Unknown World'. It was about how I didn't know anything about the world I was living in. I had come to this big city as a naive girl from a remote village. Much of what I had been taught about life was completely false. It made me feel like an alien.

I also did some art and dance classes, but my favorite was the self-defense class. I was obsessed with that class. Once I broke a thick piece of wood with a karate chop. The teacher said, "Take out all your anger, Hit it hard!". That was easy. I had a lot of anger.

I was heartbroken when I learned that the three older girls rescued with us had run away from their shelter in Haldia district. They ran back to the brothel. They didn't trust the rescue. They felt there was no way out. One of those girls, my aunt, is still in India, working in the red light area.

I am so grateful that I got to go to Sanlaap to recover. There are many shelters in Kolkata, but that place was special. That was where I first learned to trust people. I learned to read and write, and I learned that I had rights, and value as a human being.

Chapter 16

A year after I was rescued, I testified in front of the judge in court, along with three of my friends. We ourselves decided to give that statement. No one asked us to do it. I went into a room with just one lady judge, and I told her everything that had happened to me. Three others did the same. Even the IJM counselors had to wait outside. That judge was very respectful, not aggressive or harsh. She was soft-spoken and it was easy to talk to her, even about the most personal things. Because I had learned to write and read a little, I was able to sign my written testimony in front of the judge. Each time I took a step like this, I saw more hope of a new life.

Later more girls from our group decided to give their testimonies. We went many times to the court, but we were never presented in front of a jury. Mostly we talked to the judge individually. One time, we were called to identify one of the brothel managers, Rajesh. He had been caught when we were rescued, along with his wife. He was one of the ones who used to take money from customers and write in our little notebooks when we took a customer.

We all went into the prison grounds, three or four at a time, to identify him. There was a line-up of ten guys, all more or less the same age, size and type. We had to recognize the manager from that group. There was no two-way mirror between us and the guys. They could see us, plain as day.

All of the prisoners, men and women, could see us too. It made me quite nervous that it was so out in the open.

Many of us were able to identify Rajesh, the brothel manager. The only girls who couldn't recognize him were the ones who were in the brothel for only a short period of time. The police would trick us by having the guys change their clothes, or their position in the line, but we could never forget the face of someone who caused us so much pain. Rajesh's face and all the other traffickers' faces were burned into my memory.
Rajesh went to prison based on our testimony. He was Indian, unlike the other managers, who were Nepali. We heard later that he got some sickness in jail, and somehow got an early release.

In the early days, we hated going to court. We were made to go, and we felt awful every time. But as we came to grasp the wrongness of what had been done to us, we started wanting to fight for justice. We wanted to file cases against traffickers, so we could save other girls. We were becoming activists. Gradually I began to look forward to my days in court, where I could speak the truth and people would listen.

"You can use your voice as a sword, as well as a shield,"Smita told us.

I didn't understand her at first. Later I came to understand what she meant. You can use your voice to defend yourself, and you can also, actively, use it to fight against injustice, to fight for your rights and the rights of others.

The court was always changing the dates for our appearances. Often we would go all the way to the courthouse in Haldia, only to have them tell us to come back in a few weeks, or in six months. Smita told us that our case was the first case the IJM team had pursued in Haldia. Several people told her at the outset, 'There had never been a conviction for trafficking in Haldia, so Good Luck to you!'.

A lady named Pinky had been arrested along with Rajesh. There were two Pinkys at the brothel. One was Nepali Pinky, who was a really cruel person. She used to allow two or three guys to go in with little Ashayana. Two would hold her down while one of them raped her. That Pinky had lost her humanity.

When we heard that a lady named Pinky had been arrested, we were excited to testify against her, because we thought it was that cruel lady. But it was actually Indian Pinky. Indian Pinky was not a cruel person. She was like us. Even though her husband was a manager, she still had to serve customers. She was herself a victim, not a perpetrator.

A few other people were also arrested in our case, but they ran away before they were convicted. In the end, three people were brought to trial and convicted.

I felt good about taking an active role in my case, but I was always hoping the case would finish so that I could go back to Nepal. The more time passed, the more intense my longing became. Much as I appreciated my safe home at Sanlaap, I yearned for my own homeland, to speak in my native language, and to walk freely in nature. I longed for the mountains and tall trees, the dusting of snow and the open skies of my country.

I was desperate to go home, but I was worried too, because I had no idea where I would go or what I would do when I got there.

Chapter 17

When Silvio and Rose Silva were young pastors in Brazil, they always had the tendency to look after children. They always felt that the church should be about more than preaching and praying. They felt that as Christians, it was their responsibility to take people in and care for them inside their own home.

In 1996, the Silvas were living in Goiania, the capital city of Brazil, with their toddler son, David. Silvio was 32, wiry and full of energy. He was talkative and always making jokes. Rose was 26, shyer and quieter, but equally strong minded and tireless. Brazilians are very diverse in their physical appearance, and the Silva family was the perfect example. Rose had porcelain skin, light eyes and hair, and the soft features of a German farm girl, Silvio had the dark eyes, dark hair and coloring of his Portuguese ancestors, and David was Afro-Brazilian.

There were three girls coming to their church whose mother was an alcoholic and whose father had abandoned them. One day the oldest girl called Silvio and said, "I have no place to go. My grandmother left me on the street".

Silvio and Rose went to pick her up, expecting just to pick up one child, but there she was with her two sisters. The family's apartment was small, but they couldn't turn the girls away, so they decided to foster them. David came and slept on the floor of Rose and Silvio's room, and the three sisters moved into his bedroom.

Soon after the girls moved in, Dr. José Rodrigues came to speak at Silvio and Rose's church. He spoke about a dead girl on the sidewalk in Mumbai. Dr. José had gone to a Mumbai red light area, where he had been invited to set up a health clinic. One day, walking through the red light area, he came across the body of a girl lying in the street. She was about twelve years old, naked and wrapped in a thin sheet.

Then a garbage truck came. The garbagemen picked up the girl's body and threw it in their truck.

Dr. José was shocked and horrified, but other bystanders just shrugged and turned away. They didn't understand his distress. "She's just a Nepali whore," they said. They could not see her humanity.

Dr. José got the dream at that moment to create a pathway out of sex trafficking for Nepali girls. He came back to Brazil, talking to anyone who would listen about that girl on the sidewalk. He came to the Silvas' church and shared the story, crying as he told it.

Silvio thought *'Okay, it's a terrible thing, but what is our business with girls in Nepal? This old guy is crying, but what is the point? It has nothing to do with me'*. He was moved by the story, but not enough to drop everything and move to Nepal.

A few years passed. Dr. José returned to the church in 1998 and spoke again about the girl. "We must do something!" he told the congregation.

A couple from the church volunteered to go to Nepal, and Silvio offered that the church would support them financially.

Silvio and Rose had built a comfortable life for themselves in Goiania. They had a nice car, and they had finally upgraded to a bigger apartment. Life was good, but they had begun to feel less fulfilled in the church work they were doing. So, they made the decision to go and serve in Africa.

Dr. José came to see them, saying, "Please don't go to Africa. Go to Nepal. That couple that you sent from your church, they never actually went. The girls of Nepal need you!"

At that moment, Silvio felt God speaking to him, saying *'I don't want that couple from your church. I don't want your money, or your church's money, I want you to go to Nepal'*.
Rose felt the same calling, so they decided to go.

Forty-five days later, in November 2000, the family was on a plane to Nepal. They were totally unprepared, speaking not a word of Nepali or English.

"I actually thought Nepal was a state in India," Rose admitted. "I had no sense of the geography, no idea of the culture. I had never been outside of Brazil. Someone gave me an almanac and it had exactly one paragraph about Nepal. So I knew it had sugarcane, rice, Mount Everest, Buddhists and Hindus. That was all I knew. Oh, and I knew it was cold, and winter would soon arrive there. And there we were in the summer in the hottest city of Brazil trying to find warm clothes to take to Nepal!"

When they arrived in Kathmandu, Rose felt that someone had dropped her in by parachute and left her in this strange place. There was one guy there to meet the couple, but he flew back to Brazil after just a couple of days. The Silvas were left in a hotel, with little money, no one to advise them, and no idea where to begin. Kathmandu seemed like a frontier town, with few modern conveniences.

"I don't know how we survived," said Rose. "That guy left some people to help us but they were the worst people ever! They were cheating us, doing everything bad to us, trying to make us go back to Brazil. We had to learn English, learn Nepali, and until we did, we had no way to communicate".

Rose devoted herself to learning Nepali as quickly as possible, but she could find no teacher to help her, as her only language was Portuguese. She studied on her own and picked up whatever she could from whoever would help her - the waiter at the hotel, the lady at the grocery market, anybody.

Just before Rose came to Nepal, she had felt really scared about going because she had never been outside of Brazil. She asked God, '*What do you want me to do there in Nepal?*' She heard a strong message back. '*Just be a mother. Nothing more than that*'. She worried that she wouldn't know how to be a mother to trafficked girls in Nepal, where she didn't know the culture, and could not begin to understand what the girls had endured. But she was determined to give her all.

Usually when people go abroad to serve, they prepare and study for years. They learn the language and understand the culture, geography, people, and challenges of the place where they are going. They are prepared for whatever they will encounter there. Rose and Silvio's version was totally spontaneous, and not prepared at all, so they endeavored to approach everything with an open mind and a humble attitude. "We didn't come in thinking we had all the answers, and I think, in our case, that was a good thing," said Rose.

The first forty-five days in Nepal, living in a budget hotel with a six-year-old, were high in stress and low in pleasure. There was loud Nepali club music blaring every night until early morning. The Silvas hadn't known that they were staying in the middle of a party district. The hotel cost just $10 a day, which was all they could afford. They cleaned their own room because David had very bad asthma and the carpets and dust could make him very sick.

In the rush of leaving Brazil, they had lost David's asthma medicine, and didn't know if or where they could buy it in Kathmandu. One day, David did get really sick and the parents were frantic. Silvio went out at night to look for medicine. By some miracle, the asthma medicine had the same name in Nepal as in Brazil. That was not usually the case, and it saved David's life. Silvio and Rose took courage from this, to carry on, despite a rough beginning.

After a month, the Silvas began to get girls referred to them by other agencies. Two years later, they were caring for six girls in their home. They decided to call the project Apple of God's Eyes, because they wanted the girls to feel beloved and special.

The Silvas were told that the six girls were trafficking survivors. Their translator told them that one of the girls had been trafficked into a Maoist guerrilla camp where she was abused by all the guerrilla soldiers. They shared this information in their monthly reports home to Brazil, to Dr. José and the other people supporting their project. Their donors in Brazil used to cry reading these tragic stories, and one Brazilian family actually adopted one of the girls.

After a year in Kathmandu, Silvio hired a new translator. It was then that he discovered that the first translator had made all the girls' stories up! The entire time, the translator and the agencies that had referred the girls, had been lying, taking advantage of the fact that Silvio and Rose didn't speak Nepali and were just learning the culture.

The new translator asked the girls some questions about being trafficked. "What are you talking about?!" they said.

It turned out that none of the six girls had ever been trafficked. They came from poor families, and they had come to live with the Silvas because they were promised they would get a good education. Only one of the six had been a victim of sexual abuse, but she was never trafficked.

"Of course, we were so happy for them, that they had not had to endure the horror of sex trafficking," said Silvio. "But we were mortified that we ourselves had been unknowingly lying to our supporters in Brazil".

Silvio immediately called MCM, Dr. Jose's agency in Brazil that had been supporting the project. He told them the hard truth that he had just learned. Their response was that the project was a failure. The Silvas had been in Nepal for two years and had failed to achieve the goal of caring for survivors of trafficking. Silvio and Rose were told to close the doors of the home and return to Brazil immediately. The dream was crashing down.

Chapter 18

Feeling sad and defeated, the Silvas restored the girls to their families, in cases where this was possible. There were still three girls who had nowhere to go, so Silvio and Rose let them stay in the apartment, hiring a local woman to cook and watch out for them. Silvio and Rose felt terrible about leaving behind these girls who had become like family. The girls were sobbing and saying "You are my father and mother. Please, please don't go".

It was a terrible time for Rose and Silvio. Their reputation was damaged and their integrity was being questioned. No one trusted them, in Nepal, or in Brazil either. Everything they had worked so hard to build seemed to be falling apart.

Their supervisor in Brazil suggested they give their furniture to the three girls, who could sell it and use the money to survive. They were told to give up the lease on their apartment. MCM was no longer interested in financing the project.

However, Silvio didn't give up the lease. Instead, he agreed to return to Brazil on one condition: that they buy him a round trip ticket. When he got back to Brazil, a pastor friend gave him some money from a CD that some people had recorded to raise money for anti-trafficking efforts. It was $2400.

"All this money I can give you, but I cannot promise you another dollar after this," the pastor told Silvio. "All the Board members are against you returning to Nepal because your project is a failure. But if you want to take this money, you can take it and try again to do something in Nepal".

With very little money, and no moral support, it was not a promising situation. But at least Silvio had a ticket back to Kathmandu and $2400 in cash. It was enough money to survive for two months. And in those two months, things began to turn around.

Some friends from a Brazilian congregation in the USA decided to support the project. The Silvas disconnected from the people who had tricked them. They found and hired a brilliant and dedicated young woman, Mamata Tamang, who they knew from their church. They moved to a bigger apartment in another part of the city. From that point, the project started to thrive.

There was a gang in Kathmandu that forced children to beg. Every evening, the gang members would come and take all the money the kids had collected. Rose took on that gang, and rescued many girls from them, bringing them into her home.

One of those girls was Eliza. She was about 12, and had already been surviving on the streets for years. She heard about the Silvas' home and came to ask if she could stay there. At that point the home was already over capacity, so Silvio told her, "You can be the next one. As soon as we have room, you can come".

Eliza pointed at the balcony, and replied, "I would rather sleep on your balcony than alone on the streets. It will be cold and the concrete will be hard, but at least I will be safe. At least I will be close to you guys. You wouldn't have to feed me, I can take care of myself. Please just let me stay with you".

Of course, they found a way to take Eliza in, not on the balcony but inside the house.

At Christmas, Rose and Silvio couldn't afford to buy presents for all the kids, but they got a good deal on socks and mittens from the market, a nice warm wool. They divided them up so each girl got one sock and one mitten, and they could either take turns and share with each other or switch the sock and mitten between their own hands and feet. The girls were so joyful to get these simple gifts.

"I will never forget their joy," said Silvio. "It was the ultimate lesson in gratitude. It sounds unreal, like something out of a fairy tale, but that truly was our reality in the early days".

The girls were thriving, but funding the project was still a huge challenge. By the end of the year, they were once again broke. Silvio had to borrow money from a staff member to pay the rent.

Once again, Silvio and Rose discussed the possibility of closing the home. But they hated the idea of giving up. They were now working with extremely traumatized girls. They were seeing the healing power of love transforming the girls' lives. They prayed for a miracle that would allow them to keep working in Nepal.

Over the three years Silvio had been in Nepal, he had been collecting trafficking stories from articles in the newspaper. He decided to write a book based on those stories, which he published in Brazil. He didn't want to exploit survivors by asking them to retell their stories, so he shared stories that had already been told, adding insight from all that he had seen and learned in Nepal. He finished the book in just three days. The book turned out to be quite successful, and it raised thousands of dollars which got the Silvas through their funding crisis.

The book also got into hands of some precious new friends, such as Jolian, the pastor of a Brazilian church in Pennsylvania. The church community became generous and loyal donors. Their generosity was inspiring because most of the members of that congregation were recent immigrants to America who worked in construction or housekeeping. They didn't make a lot of money, but what they had, they shared with Rose and Silvio's girls, month after month and year after year.

The first thing Silvio did with these new donations was to pay for all the girls to move from government schools to private schools. The teachers in the government schools were very disrespectful and shaming towards the girls. Teachers would single girls out and talk about their backgrounds in front of the whole class. Sometimes the schools would refuse to admit girls, saying they would be a bad influence on other students. Teachers would make the girls stand up and put their hands out for inspection. If their nails were not perfectly trimmed and clean, the teacher would cane their hands or smack their ears. This humiliating treatment made the girls afraid to go to school. It was a huge improvement in their lives when they were able to go to private schools.

Over time, Apple of God's Eyes got more supporters and many more girls, including trafficking survivors returned from India. They rented more houses so they could take in more girls. They cultivated leaders from within Nepal who began to run things. In 2009 they started their own school. That made it easier to integrate girls returning from India who were many years behind in their education.

In the loving environment of Apple, girls healed from the trauma of their past, and thrived. Some of the older girls appealed to Silvio and Rose to expand the project to include boys - their brothers back in the villages - who had no hope of a positive future if they stayed at home.

Today, out of the first group of girls who lived at Apple, Raquel is a nurse in England. Promila is a doctor. Eliza, Gleiva and Marcia, and several other 'first generation' girls are on the executive team of Apple of God's Eyes.

Rose never wavered from her vision that a loving family environment, not a shelter, was what survivors needed most. "My calling here was to be a mother, not a social worker," she said. "A mother is not someone who works so many hours and then goes home. It's a twenty-four-hour job. You give yourself completely. We lived with girls in our own home for the first eight years, through the misunderstandings, visa problems, financial problems, but always as a family. The concept of family was built very strongly inside our house. I was there twenty-four hours a day for them, teaching them, loving them, listening to them, correcting them when they misbehaved, letting them do my hair, watching TV, doing schoolwork with them, just like any other family. Without boundaries. Of course, I would take time to myself, but only to keep from going crazy. But I was always available if they needed me".

"We taught all the leaders in our organization these family values," she added. "And when people don't live according to these principles, I am the lion who fights hard to restore the values. We never set out to be a shelter home or an institution of any kind. It would be so much easier to just be a social worker, providing food, shelter, education, rules and basic care. I can't do that and I don't do that. When the girls do right, I am the first one to praise them, to celebrate them. And when they do wrong, I am there to teach them, to be upset with them, to say 'You can do better'. This is a job that no one wants. This is why the government creates institutions, because creating a family requires your whole heart, your whole soul. I know we are not perfect here. We have lots of mistakes and failures, but at least these values we never give up on. You need to be there for each other, you need to fight for each other. And I love when I see the kids fighting for each other, calling each other sister and brother, and taking the pain from each other. I almost destroyed some schools here in Kathmandu, fighting for my children. That gave my girls a sense of belonging, that someone was willing to fight for them".

"Now my babies are in their twenties and I see that they hold that feeling, that strength inside their heart. Somebody was there for them... That is what heals the soul of a human being, knowing they are loved. Of course now we have professional counseling, and we are grateful for that, but we didn't always have that. The counseling center was my kitchen counter. I would be cooking and the girls would come home from school and pour out their hearts and their hurts. We had a soul connection. They gave me their fear and their pain, and I gave it up to God. And somehow it was enough".

Other homes for rescued girls have armed guards, fences, and electric gates. Apple of God's Eyes had nothing like that. They didn't even have locks on the gates. Rose and Silvio always said, "We have only a fence of love and if that is not enough, nothing will be enough".

Chapter 19

I had lived for almost two years at Sanlaap, when the IJM team brought some new girls to the shelter, who they had just rescued. Among them was my cousin. She brought a whole heap of unwelcome news. Apparently, my mother was very depressed and crying all the time. My cousin thought that my mother had some kind of disease inside her. Our aunt had fallen from a cliff and died. My brother was still hanging out with wrong people.

I was sad and very conflicted. I cried a lot but once again, it was all out of my control. I ached to be with my mother, or at least to be back in Nepal. I was desperate for my court case to finish, so I could go home to my own country and people. It felt like a weight on my chest all the time.

Gradually, I was able to channel my homesickness and frustration into something more constructive. I became even more focused on my dream, to save more sisters, the children from our area who would be trafficked if no one intervened. I wanted many more girls to be saved from the nightmare of brothel life, and to get the same wonderful opportunities that I was getting.

Even though the court case took a long time, the IJM team kept us well informed. They explained what was happening every step of the way and shared everything they were doing on our behalf. They gave us hope, but also, they were honest and realistic.

For the first time in a trafficking repatriation, the Nepalese government had gotten involved. They had to identify that we were indeed Nepali citizens, before they would allow us to return home. That took some time. Case workers back in Nepal had to go to each of our villages and find families or local officials who could confirm our identities. Because we all came from these remote and disorderly places, this took a long time. It seemed kind of unfair. No one cared when we left Nepal to go to India, but then we had to prove that we had a right to go back to our own country.

One time the counselors brought a brochure from a place called Apple of God's Eyes. They explained that it was an organization in Kathmandu that cared for survivors and children who were in danger of being trafficked. It looked impossibly beautiful, with large, sky-blue houses, and smiling children. The children looked well-dressed and healthy. They didn't have the scrappy, startled look of children in a shelter home. That brochure made me hope that I could someday live there, in one of those beautiful sky-blue houses.

In June 2010, after living at Sanlaap for twenty months, we finally got the news we had been hoping for. Someone came from IJM to tell us "You are really going home. In one week!"

Not only was I finally going home, but I was actually going to live at Apple of God's Eyes.

Smita and Rupa took us to a shopping mall to buy new clothes. At Sanlaap, we had earned some money doing household chores and selling handmade cards that we made from leaves. We had worked for nearly two years and earned a little money every day. Sanlaap gave us all the money we had been saving, IJM added some money to it, and we used it to buy new clothes and suitcases.

Once we had permission to return to our homeland, Smita had to figure out the logistics of transporting so many girls from India to Nepal. We couldn't take an international flight, because we had no passports. There was a huge security risk as well. Trafficking rings are a form of organized crime. They can be quite vicious and cunning, and their network is far-reaching. It extends into the police and border patrol.

Ultimately, they decided on a plane and train combination. We would drive for three hours, then take a train to the border and cross from India into Nepal. There, eleven of us would be handed over into the custody of Apple of God's Eyes, and four would be placed with another organization. Then we would all take a short domestic flight to Kathmandu.

I was afraid to get too excited. I had been disappointed before, many times. The night before we left, the housemother came and told us, "You are leaving tomorrow morning". We stayed up all night in anticipation.

On the morning of June 30, 2010, we made our beds at Sanlaap for the last time and carried our luggage down to the courtyard. All the girls and housemothers, and my dear teachers Chanda and Grandfather were there to see us off with tears in their eyes. Sanlaap's founder Indrani was there too. They hugged and kissed us. Some people gave speeches. Some were sobbing so hard, they could not speak.

Everyone at Sanlaap loved the Nepali girls because we don't fight and argue. We are peaceful types. So everyone loved us, girls and staff. The emotional goodbye lasted over an hour, and then we got into the cars, and drove out those big iron gates for the last time.

The first time I had walked through those gates, I was full of dread, and devoid of hope. I was sure I was walking into a prison, or some different kind of brothel. Little did I know it would be such a place of healing and for me, the first step to a normal life.

We were being repatriated in two groups over two days. I was in the first group. We traveled all day and night by train. On the train, Smita tried to distract me from my worries by showing me a video made by a few Nepali girls at Apple. They were sharing their stories, which were similar to mine, and saying that they had the dream to work against human trafficking, to work in the villages, to create awareness. At that moment my eyes filled with tears because I thought that I was alone in wanting to speak out against trafficking. After watching the video, I realized that there were many people standing with me. I was not alone in wanting to change my society.

Chapter 20

Like me, Mamata Tamang comes from the Tamang ethnic group. However, her life journey was very different from mine because her parents had more resources, and because they were committed to her getting an education. Mamata was born a few hours outside Kathmandu. Her parents worked in a carpet factory. Then her parents moved to Bhaktapur, a little closer to the city, to open their own small carpet factory.

When Mamata was thirteen, she saw a series about human trafficking on television. It told the stories of many girls trafficked for different reasons into brothels. Watching this, Mamata was very distressed and also very inspired. She decided she would work for such girls when she grew up. The series lasted for three months with weekly episodes. In the last episode, a real trafficking activist came on, to talk about her work with survivors. That lady became Mamata's hero. Mamata hoped that one day she could be like that lady, helping trafficked girls to become free.

Mamata's parents were Christian so she used to go to church as a child. When she was sixteen years old, a girl whose parents worked in the carpet factory told her about a church opened by some foreigners. There, she met Silvio and Rose, and they hired her to do some translation work. After graduating from college, she came to live and work full time at Apple of God's Eyes.

Over the years, Mamata gained many more skills and her leadership in the organization grew. By 2009, she was serving as the Chairperson of the organization. Mamata's feisty, no-nonsense personality and grit served her well when she went to India to fight in the courts for Nepali survivors. She helped many survivors come home. She also fought for girls' rights in the Nepali courts. Mamata fought hard to get us home, and into her home, at Apple of God's Eyes.

Back in 2008, when our rescue happened. Don was actually in Nepal, visiting Apple. He was with Mamata, tracking the progress of the raid by cell phone. He got so excited about how many girls were being rescued. Mamata got excited too, listening to him share moment by moment updates of the raid.

Soon after the rescue, the Apple of God's Eyes team was enlisted to do home studies on the girls who had been rescued. Mamata had to find out how each family was, whether they were involved in trafficking their daughter. She had to decide if it was safe for the girl to return to her family, or if they were involved in trafficking her, or so destitute that she would always be at risk.

Mamata went to Nuwakot with Silvio and Rose and another Apple staff member to conduct the home studies. They went to the police station to ask for help with the girls' files in their hands. The police called someone from another organization in the area to help, because that local organization's staff knew the area well. The lady they called tried to avoid coming to the police station. She wanted to stay away from the matter, but the police insisted that she come. When the lady finally showed up, she did not want to get involved. Because the police were pressuring her, she eventually said, "Oh the people in this area are wild. They don't want to be disturbed about trafficking. You should just leave them alone".

The Apple team felt that something was fishy. The next day, they sent Bhuvan, a young male staff member, to meet with that lady at her office. The lady asked to borrow Bhuvan's cell phone and used it to call the main trafficker of the area. The trafficker she called is a local guy from my own village. We call him Diamond Dan, because of the diamond pinky ring he wears, and because he has become rich from the sale of many young girls.

Because the lady had called Diamond Dan from Bhuvan's phone, the trafficker had Bhuvan's phone number. Diamond Dan called Bhuvan later that day, and asked "When are the girls coming back from India? I need to know".

Bhuvan did not know that the person who had called him was a trafficker, but when Diamond Dan came to meet him, Bhuvan recognized him, and managed to escape.

The Apple team spent two months trying to get to the bottom of the situation. Bhuvan was suspended for a couple of months to determine whether he was involved with the traffickers. Eventually, the team learned that Bhuvan's phone number had been given to the trafficker by the lady from the local organization, working for a larger international organization. She pretended to be asking Diamond Dan for help, but was in fact collaborating with him. Mamata and Silvio spoke out publicly about the corruption of the local organization, and got in big trouble for it.

Unfortunately, situations like this are all too common in my area. The community, the police, judges and even local charities collaborate with the traffickers. Almost everyone in the village helps to protect the system of trafficking. The buyers and sellers and those who help them profit from the system, while girls' lives are destroyed. The coin that pays for my community's way of life is the suffering of children.

While in Nuwakot District, the team did a home study on the youngest girl in our group, Ashayana, who was ten when we were rescued. I don't know how long she had been in the brothel, but she was already there when I came. When Bhuvan talked to Ashayana's father, the father said "What are you doing?! Why are you trying to bring my girl back? Look around you. Nothing grows in this altitude. We need her money. Don't bring her back".

"But she is in the brothel, she is in trouble, she is your daughter," said Bhuvan.

Ashayana's father could not look Bhuvan in the eyes when he replied. "If you bring her back, I will not accept her. I will only sell her again".

Six months later, Mamata was sent to Kolkata because there were some girls in our group whose background information did not match up. She brought the home study reports to Sanlaap to clear up the confusion.

"As soon as I met the girls, we recognized each other, we already felt a connection," said Mamata. "We all shared a common surname *(Tamang)* and spoke the same language *(again, Tamang)*. We asked each other questions like 'which sub-caste are you from?' and 'which village are you from?' We felt a kinship. We are all Tamang, so we are all sisters. I wanted very much to bring my sisters home, and into my home".

Mamata had been thinking about us since the day we got rescued. She had been working through Nepali and Indian government agencies for us to be placed at Apple. But the home placement decision can be extremely political. If one organization has a relationship with the government agency in charge of the repatriation, girls will get placed there. Usually in high profile cases like ours, girls get placed in larger organizations.

But Mamata and everyone at Apple felt strongly that we were their sisters. They already cared a lot about us, and they believed we would thrive with them. At that time, Mamata was only twenty-four years old. She is small of stature, and people would often think she was a young girl, and not take her seriously. So she did not feel not confident that she would be able to get us placed at Apple. But after meeting us in Kolkata, she knew she had to find a way.

There were a lot of hurdles to overcome, for getting us home. Immediately after the rescue raid, the Child Welfare Commission in Kolkata informed the Nepali Consulate in Kolkata of the situation. A home study was ordered, and that was when things got a little crazy, with Bhuvan and the corrupt local organization and Diamond Dan.

Mamata gave the home study reports to the Nepali Consulate in India, which then processed each case with the Foreign Affairs Office in Nepal. Once a girl was proved to be a Nepali citizen, the repatriation process could begin. Then Apple of God's Eyes, as the receiving home, had to submit documents proving that they were able to care for the girls properly.

While it is true that many people were involved in trafficking us, more were involved in rescuing us and getting us home. Thanks to all those brave and persistent people, we were finally on our way home.

We spent one night on the train, sleeping a few hours at a time, but too excited to stay asleep for long. In the morning, we got off the train at the border between India and Nepal. I was exhausted and more than a little anxious about what would happen next. I was very happy to see the familiar face of Mamata there, to meet us and to take custody of us.

We had a quick reunion, but it was very rushed because next we had to deal with the border police. Before crossing the border into Nepal, we had to register on the India side and get permission to leave. The border police station looked like an office but felt like a courtroom. The officers were asking our stories, wanting to hear the details. They asked us some really inappropriate questions, like "How many men did you sleep with?" "What did you do for them?" "Did you enjoy it?"

They were laughing while they asked us these horrible questions. It was embarrassing for us, and distressing for the adults. Mamata kept calm, but I could see she was enraged by the officers' behavior.

I was furious that they didn't want to let us go back to our own country. When I was taken from Nepal to India, it wasn't hard at all. No one asked a thing. And now we needed to ask permission just to go home? Every girl had to give a testimony about what happened to her. We had nothing to eat. Smita and Mamata were running all over the place, trying to manage the situation. It was getting close to the time of our plane departure. I became worried that we would miss our flight and I would have to stay longer in India.

We were finally allowed through, but on the Nepal side, there were yet more obstacles to overcome. The District Officer in charge was not sensitized at all about trafficking. "These foolish girls went of their own accord to India,because they thought they could get rich in prostitution," he said. "And now they want to come back, causing all these problems".

Nepal can be very bureaucratic. There were endless papers to be signed and rubber-stamped. The Officer seemed to be taking pleasure in making us wait, in holding his power over us. I had seen this kind of behavior many times before, especially in the red light area. People who feel small try to make themselves bigger by finding the most powerless person and pushing her even further down. Often the most powerless person is a girl.

The process took such a long time, we almost missed the plane. We had to take a car twenty minutes across town, driving very fast indeed. Thankfully they did hold the plane for us, for thirty minutes. All the other passengers were already sitting on the plane waiting when we finally got there.

That was my first time on an airplane. I felt a little scared at take-off and landing. But it was also quite fascinating and strange to see clouds below us rather than above. The airplane took us to Kathmandu in just thirty minutes. Mamata sat beside me, holding my hand and talking softly the whole time. I was rather agitated from all the questioning and rushing to catch our flight. Before I knew it, we were landing in Kathmandu.

I used to think that to return to Nepal was an impossible thing, but the impossible had become possible. As I climbed down the airplane steps and into the cool air of Kathmandu (at an altitude of 4,600 feet), I was overwhelmed with so many different emotions. I could not hold back my tears.

They were tears of joy and relief, that after four years, I was finally home. They were tears of grief for the lost years and for the brutality I experienced in India. They were tears of homesickness, for my familiar room and friends at Sanlaap. They were bitter tears of longing for my mother and father, who could not be there to welcome me.

I was surrounded by people, including many who I knew and loved. And yet in that moment, I felt alone, untethered, a girl without a family, a purpose or a plan.

Hope and fear were fighting for space inside me, jumbled up with wounds, deep and old. Mamata must have noticed my hesitation, because she put her arm around my waist and hugged me close, like a sister.

I took strength from her hug, wiped my tears on my scarf, and with my small but mighty sister by my side, I stepped out onto the runway into my new life.

Chapter 21

When we stepped out the door of the airport, there arose a loud cheer. A group of girls from Apple of God's Eyes was waiting for us. They welcomed us with warm hugs and much affection. They hung a garland of flowers and a white *katha* scarf around each of our necks. They held up a large paper sign that they had made for us. On it was written each of our names, and the words 'WELCOME HOME'.

We all piled into a van. I felt grateful that by this point I was used to traveling by car, so I did not throw up and spoil the magic of the moment.

The van took me to a house where an even larger group of people was waiting to welcome me. "We are your family," they told me. "We have been waiting for you".

As we stepped out of the van, children sang a song of welcome and rushed to hug us. There were many small girls, teenage boys and girls, and adults, both Nepalis and foreigners. I searched the crowd to see if there was someone from my village. I was hoping there would be, and there was. One of my relatives, Payel, was there, and also two other girls from my area. One of those girls I had actually met in India, when I was first brought to the brothel. My aunt Payel was two or three years older than me, the other two girls were about my age, fifteen.

It was a little surprising to have so many people I had never met coming to hug me. They draped even more garlands and khatas around our necks and led us inside. They led us to chairs and asked us to sit down. Then the sisters of the home danced and sang to welcome us. When I saw these girls dancing, something cracked open in my heart, and hope rushed in.

I thought, *'These girls are doing all kinds of things. Maybe I could also learn something here and do something for my village. Opportunities are here. Maybe life will not turn out to be as bad as I expected'.*

Boys from the Apple boys' home had also prepared a song to perform for us. The leaders had included the boys in the welcome ceremony because they didn't want us to be afraid that there were boys and men there, in the Apple family. They wanted to show us that boys and men could be kind, not just using and abusing.

During the welcome ceremony, they gave me a lot of gifts - sweets, dried fruit and chocolates, a school uniform and a school bag. The principal of the Apple school was there and she told me I would soon be going to school.

Meeting these people and feeling their love, I felt that I had at last found a family where I would be safe and accepted. I felt joy and relief being back in my own country, where everyone was speaking Nepali. I got a warm feeling, like when you walk into your house after a long, hard day, take off your shoes and put down your heavy bags.

My dream of returning to Nepal had come true, so maybe other dreams could also come true. The world I grew up in was just bitterness and tears, people using each other to get what they wanted. The world which I was seeing at Apple was hope, selfless love and warm hugs. At first it was difficult for me to completely believe and trust it, but I came to know that it was real. Their love never wavered.

After finishing the program, we ate a meal that they had prepared for us, with all our favorite foods. I was practically falling asleep over my plate. It had been such an emotional day and I had barely slept on the train the night before, or at Sanlaap the night before that.

We girls were divided among the different Apple homes. I was going to live at Home Three, and three other girls from my group would be joining me there when they arrived the following day. Mamata was one of the leaders of Home Three. Because she was a familiar face, they decided to put me in her home. Each home was like a different family, with its own personality, its own routines, its own way of dealing with problems, and its own challenges.

They took me by van to Home Three, where yet another large group of sisters was waiting for me, even though it was quite late. Again, they all hugged and welcomed me. I was overjoyed to learn that my aunt, Payel, was also living in that home, and that she would be one of my roommates. That was very comforting to me. Payel spoke Tamang. I have known her since childhood.

The IJM counselors always used to tell us, "You will go home to Nepal and live at Apple of God's Eyes." They showed us pictures and that brochure many times. By the time I was repatriated, I had heard the name Apple of

God's Eyes hundreds of times. But still it was hard to believe that I was actually there.

In my village, everyone lived in small rustic houses, and when I was brought to India, I was kept inside old, crumbling buildings, surrounded by more moldy and crumbling buildings. And then I lived in a large shelter home, which was clean and decent, but basic. I had never been inside a beautiful house like the ones at Apple of God's Eyes. It was a three-story building, sky blue with white trim. Home Three had about thirty girls living in it, and every inch of space was used. But it seemed like a mansion to me.

My bedroom was so beautiful. There were two bunk beds, with pink and white sheets. The beds were covered with dolls and stuffed animals. Despite being desperately tired, I fell asleep very late that night. My mind was cluttered. I felt hopeful for the future, and excited. I was also a bit unsettled to be in a new place and missing my friends and familiar home at Sanlaap.

On the second day, the entire welcome program was repeated for the next group of girls arriving from India. On the third day, we went to see the Apple school. I was especially excited about going to a real school for the first time in eight years, because I had just been doing informal school at Sanlaap. We played on the swings and looked in all the classrooms.

Next, we went to a shopping mall. I was surprised when I found out the reason we were there. We were not going to get practical items like clothes or towels. Instead, we were told to pick out our favorite doll or stuffed animal. This was Silvio's idea, and he did it for each new girl that came to

Apple, even the older girls. Silvio felt that our childhoods had been taken from us, and we probably never had a father who bought dolls for us. The dolls were meant to show us that at Apple, we were allowed to be children. We were safe. We would have the time and space to have a childhood, if that's what we wanted. I never had the chance to be a child back in the village. I was too weighed down with worry and responsibility. In the brothels, our youth was used against us.

I picked out a large stuffed dog. I named him 'Ro' which means friend in Tamang. Ro has been with me ever since, and his fur has soaked up a lot of tears over the years. He never complains.

Chapter 22

After the strange and wonderful shopping trip, Smita and the rest of the IJM team came to say goodbye. They were going back to India, and we would not see them again for a very long time. I felt very sad because we had become attached to them. They had walked beside us for so long. I knew it wasn't their fault they were leaving us. They had to go back to their jobs and their lives. But I didn't feel connected yet with the Apple family, and I couldn't help but feel a little abandoned. The team's departure gave me a hollow feeling that lasted for the next few days.

Thankfully, I had a lot of things to distract me from my sadness. After two years living inside a shelter, where we could only leave to go to court, all of a sudden I could walk freely. I could go outside whenever I wanted. The gates and doors were always open! There was no guard. I was quite amazed when I first saw girls from our home going to the shop to buy vegetables. I wanted very much to do that.

Outside, everything I saw was so different from what I had known before. Nepal is my home, but Kathmandu was nothing like my village. It is a large city in a valley ringed by mountains. Many of its buildings are red brick and two or three stories tall. There are lots of people and the roads are clogged with traffic, but still you get the feeling that you are at the edge of the Himalayas.

At first, I felt a little afraid of the outside. Outside life felt too big. Inside felt more normal. So many things had happened to me in the last four years. I was self-conscious, worried what people would think of me. But of course, no one around the city knew anything about me or my history. The home leaders and other girls coaxed me out, and took me all over the place, to visit the different Apple homes, and to the shops. Like any family, we had to buy vegetables and cook our food.

For the first time since I left my village, my life felt like my own. If I had been stuck inside at Apple, I would have been thinking all the time, reliving my past. Thankfully I was super busy, going out, buying things, walking all around the neighborhood, sometimes for no reason at all. I was giddy with the freedom of it. That freedom brought more healing.

Every night all of us at Home Three gathered as a family for dinner and shared what had happened that day. That was a lovely time.

A few weeks after I came to Apple,Dr. José Rodrigues was visiting from Brazil. Dr. José was the reason Apple existed. He had the dream of rescuing Nepali girls from Indian brothels and bringing them home. He was the one who sent Silvio and Rose to Nepal. Silvio invited me and the other girls to a gathering at Home Two to meet Dr. José, so he could see that his dream had indeed come true. Dr. José was getting older. I very much wanted to thank him while I had the chance.

We had all heard the story of Dr. José and the dead girl in Mumbai. Tanu and I asked if we could do a short reenactment of that story, as a way of thanking and honoring Dr. José. After our skit, I asked if I could say a few words. Everyone was surprised because we had just come back from

India, and people expected us to be still adjusting, and a little overwhelmed. But I had been silent long enough. I *was* overwhelmed, but not with distress. I was overwhelmed with the urge to speak what was in my heart.

I spoke in Nepali for ten minutes and Mamata translated into Portuguese. I said that at first I wanted to kill all the traffickers. I wanted to go to Nuwakot with a machine gun like Rambo and put everyone down. But my people do not know what they are doing. It is because of ignorance, not evil, that they sell their daughters. I shared my dream to open a project in my village, to educate people, so they wouldn't traffic their children. I explained that my intention is to go there and speak about my suffering and to teach the community, not judge them.

Dr. José started to cry so loud, people in the neighborhood could hear him. He was literally howling. His daughter was there, and she was afraid he was having a heart attack because he was crying so hard. He stopped for a second, then started to howl again. I was quite confused and had no idea why Dr. José was crying so much.

Silvio was also very moved. "All of us, we used to hate the people from that area, because they put the children into brothels," he said. "Anjali came with a different message. She asked us to forgive them, which was not part of our plan. How could somebody who had suffered like she did have such a deep understanding of forgiveness?"

"Anjali had a vision all along about changing people's mentality, through education, through love, through teaching, and that vision never changed," Rose added. "Even with all the suffering and pain, that was always her message. Sometimes our girls would get so disappointed when they went back to their village and they saw other people hadn't changed or become more aware. The girls' hearts were pure and full of love and forgiveness, and many times they came back crying, disappointed and frustrated by the lack of progress in their family and village. In Nepal, people often give up because the culture will not accept them. Anjali shared the message from the first week that you can be different. You can rebuild yourself. She showed other girls that whatever you want, whatever you believe, can happen".

Chapter 23

Starting school was one of the greatest adventures of my life. The Apple school started a new class for us called the Special Class, because many of us were starting school for the first time as teenagers. Others were returning to school after a long absence.

I had to wait a week or two for school to start, because it was a summer holiday when I arrived. I could not wait for that first day. I hadn't been inside a school for eight years. It was always my dream to go to school like a normal child, wearing a school uniform. At Sanlaap we just wore our regular clothes because classes were held at the shelter. The girls who had lived at Sanlaap longer went outside to school and wore uniforms. I always envied that. We recently rescued girls couldn't go outside to school because of the risk of traffickers snatching us and taking us back. If that happened, we would never again be found.

I loved going to school at Apple. Our classes were taught in English but explained in Nepali.

Every night in bed, I would think, what will happen next? I studied until 11:00 or 12:00 at night and woke up at 3:00 or 4:00am because I loved to study, and I had so much catching up to do. During class, when the teacher gave us work, I would do it as quickly as I could. When I arrived home, I couldn't wait to do my homework. Whatever my teacher gave me, I had to finish it all and prepare for the next day.

Not all of the girls were as in love with school as I was. Some of them were very frustrated with it. Others felt it was too late for them to catch up. They felt embarrassed to be teenagers doing kindergarten work. Some were keen to start vocational training so they could get a job and be independent or send money home to help their families. Only a few of the girls who returned from brothels in India ended up continuing all the way through high school. I was ready to do whatever it took to be one of them.

One of the happiest moments was at the end of the school year. I won an award as the most dedicated student in the school. They were distributing prizes and all these people started congratulating me. I had never heard of such a thing and had no idea what was going on.

The Special class girls, who had come back from India together, mostly hung out only with each other and didn't have friends outside our class. When the new school year started, I was no longer in the Special Class. I was put in grade six with a whole different group of kids. That was a breakthrough. I made different friends, some from the local area. The kids didn't behave differently towards me because of my background. The teachers made no distinctions either. They were frank and spoke normally to me. I could line up with all the other kids, an ordinary schoolgirl, no different from anyone else.

I was learning to adjust to life in the mainstream. As I hadn't been in school for long, and was still struggling in every subject, I always came in tenth position in my classes, or even lower. But I just kept working away, and in the final exam that year, I was able to get the third position with a score of 83%. That helped me to skip a grade and go to grade eight in my third year of school.

In the eighth grade, I was with classmates closer to my own size and age. Then I started to study even more seriously. The upper grades were harder but I managed to stay in the top 10%. But then in grade nine, I failed one exam and got a really low mark in a math class. I was devastated. But my teacher and Mamata and Rose told me to just pick myself up and keep going, so that's what I did.

School gave me a new identity. I wasn't just a village girl. I wasn't just a survivor of trafficking. I was a student. I took great pride in that identity. I learned to read and write, and now that I am literate, I can go anywhere. I can speak up for myself and others. I can read street signs, or a contract. I can write a book about my story. People say, 'knowledge is power' and I agree. I know what it is to have neither.

Through the ups and downs of school and life, Home Three was my refuge. It was such a happy place, full of energy with sisters of all ages. We were always having parties at our house. Celebrating birthdays is not something we did in the village, so that was new for me. We used to dance a lot. At Christmastime especially, there was dancing and singing every night. At *Holi* (a Nepali festival celebrating the return of spring), we threw water on each other.

In the early days, I was shy and self-conscious. Everyone else would be singing and dancing and I would just stand there awkwardly. But eventually I realized, no one is looking at me. I can dance like a crazy fool and no one cares! I could lay my burdens down for a while.

As I got older and more settled, the home leaders started to trust me with more responsibilities. That made me feel even more accepted, and useful. It gave me purpose.

Home Three was full of all these different people, with all kinds of experiences and emotions. That felt normal, like a normal family. I don't remember anyone ever pointing out to me that I was trafficked or making me feel less because of it. Even the youngest children, they never said anything about it, even by accident. Being free to grow up as a normal girl was one of the most healing things for me.

To this day, whenever I walk past my old house, I get a warm feeling.

Chapter 24

In the early days at Apple, I heard people talking about Jesus and the love of God. But as everything was so new, at first I wasn't really able to pay attention. My understanding of God unfolded slowly. The girls in my home would pray every day. They didn't use specific words. They just said what they were feeling. It was very informal. No one pressured me to pray, or taught me, 'Pray like this' or 'Do that". People used the prayer time to share their feelings as well. It was like group therapy, with God.

As the days and weeks passed, I saw the extraordinary love that these people had. They weren't perfect, they made mistakes. But they were guided by this love and light, and they always came back to it. They believed and they lived what Jesus said about showing your love for him by loving other people, especially people in need. I was drawn to that love. I wanted to learn more about it. I didn't make a decision suddenly to become a Christian. There were a lot of prayers and crying for many years. Slowly I realized that God had been walking beside me all along. Then I took some classes and learned more.

My faith journey wasn't smooth or easy. I was always crying, and asking God, *Why did this happen to me? Why did you let my father die? Why did my mother neglect me? Why did I get trafficked by my own people? No one in the village ever even told me it was wrong'*.

My prayers were mostly me crying at first. But as I grew in faith, learning about God's love. I learned that even though these awful things happened, God loves me. God was working through all these people to get me out of that situation.

Silvio always said we need to forgive those who have wronged us. We ourselves are the ones who suffer when we can't forgive. In Nepal we say that holding on to resentment is like holding onto a hot coal. It will burn and damage you, but you holding on to a hot coal will have no effect whatsoever on those who have wronged you. Although I talked about forgiving the people in my village when Dr. José was visiting, in reality, it was an ongoing challenge.

Sometimes it's still hard not to be angry and bitter about what happened to me. Forgiveness is a practice you choose every day, not a one-time thing. Still today, angry thoughts sometimes come up, and I have to choose forgiveness, again and again. It can be tiresome, but I find it is the only way I can live a happy life.

I've seen what happens when people stay stuck in their pain. They may be physically free, but their mind and spirit are still trapped in the brothel. They become their own jailers. And very often, those are the girls who run back to the red light area.

I don't like when people divide and discriminate based on faith. Christianity is the way of love. Jesus talked constantly about love and forgiveness. He uplifted and celebrated the lowly people, those at the margins. That resonates for me. I don't like to focus on our differences, or on what others are doing wrong. It's not constructive. Whatever people believe, we should win their hearts by sharing positive things, not by saying negative things about others.

I like that Christianity has no castes. No one is higher and no one is lower. Even if someone has just arrived at Apple, she is welcomed as a sister and daughter. It doesn't matter what caste she is, or if she is rich or poor, or what happened in her past.

My relationship with God was a huge part of my healing. Even after all the great counseling, I still struggled with feeling worthless. I showed a cheerful and confident face to the world, but inside I felt extremely broken, and worthless. It wasn't just the trafficking and rape, although that certainly made it worse. We were not treated as humans in the red light area. We were objects you could buy, and discard when you were done. Even before all that, I wasn't cherished by my family. My mother left me to live in a shepherd's hut, and then got married without even telling me. That left a hole in my heart that was still open and raw.

I came to believe that my value comes from God. I have worth as a human being, as a child of God. God cherishes me, and that made me value myself more. No one is worthless or broken beyond repair.

Counseling was helpful and necessary in the early stages of my recovery. But for me the deepest healing came from the freedom that I started to enjoy, from living as a normal girl in a family environment, from prayer time where I could pour out my emotion to a loving God, and from the love that was showered on me every day. Healing came from finally having a family that accepted me.

I don't believe that it was God's plan for me to be trafficked. I believe that through evil systems, greed and injustice, people tried to destroy my life. God worked miracles through many people's lives to bring me out of that terrible place, and to give me what I needed to be healed and whole.

Slowly, I started to talk, and later to write about what happened in India. Now I can speak quite openly about it. It took four or five years for me to start feeling fully healed. In that first year, I cried a lot, I needed a lot of care and support, and began to see that there was a way to move forward. Whenever I couldn't see any way out, any way around a problem, I would cry, sometimes for hours on end. All that crying really relieved my pain.

The Apple family were very open and honest. Other girls and women shared very frankly about their experiences in the brothels of India. They didn't feel ashamed to talk about it, and why should they? I learned from them that I could also share my pain and my story with people who I trusted. Sharing made everything easier to bear. When we share a burden, it automatically relieves the tension. Talking and talking made my tensions go away. Thankfully, there were many sisters who were willing to listen.

After the first couple of years, I no longer needed to cry every single night. I was able to comfort myself, and then to comfort and counsel others. And although there will always be challenges and problems in my life, as in everyone's life, I eventually got to the point where I didn't need to keep suffering from what happened in the past.

To have come from where I was to where I am today feels like an absolute miracle.

Chapter 25

Even though we were free and in a safe and loving place, often we had to fight to stay there. It seemed like someone was always trying to drag us back.

Nine months after we came to Apple, when everything was still quite new, the mother of Richa -one of the girls rescued with me - filed a case to try to get her daughter back. Richa's mother was a brothel owner in Mumbai, and Richa was trafficked to the same place as me, outside Kolkata. Her older and younger sisters were also in forced prostitution. Richa had never had much contact with her mother. She couldn't even remember what her mother looked like.

The mother came to Kathmandu with a lawyer from Mumbai, accompanied by many women from the village. She claimed that Apple of God's Eyes had stolen Richa and was not allowing her to see her own child. It was all a ruse. She never cared about her daughter. She just wanted to make more money selling her again.

Mamata recorded the interview using a hidden camera disguised as a pen. She showed the video to Richa, who said "My mother is lying about everything".

The mother filed complaints against Apple in many places, causing a lot of trouble. The Women's Commission and Human Rights Commission came to investigate, with a gun and a warrant against Mamata, as the Chairperson of the organization. Thankfully, Mamata was in Brazil at the time. Silvio brought Richa to talk to the commissioners, and once they talked with her, they saw that it was all a ruse and dropped the investigation.

Richa was greatly relieved. It wasn't safe for her back in her village. The thought of being re-trafficked was unbearable. For a while after that incident, we all had to be more careful, and stay inside more until the issue was resolved. There was a serious concern that Richa's mom and goons from her village would try to kidnap Richa and other girls from our group, now that they knew where to find us.

Mamata helped Richa to argue her own case in court. She testified that she wanted to stay at Apple and continue her education. Back in the village, she would have no opportunities and could easily be trafficked again. We were all so relieved when she won her case and was able to stay.

We were happy for Richa, and also for ourselves, because if one family was able to take their daughter back, then it would surely have led to other families doing the same. We had learned about our human rights, we had been sensitized, but back in the village, nothing had changed. Trafficking was still the status quo.

The following year, the Indian court summoned me to Kolkata to identify a person who was the owner of the brothel building when I was there. I lost a whole month of school, and I found it terribly stressful to be back in

Kolkata, a place with many unhappy memories. It was frustrating because I didn't even get the opportunity to identify the guy. That was a tough year because I failed in two things. I failed one of my subjects in school and I failed to complete the identification.

Sometimes Smita would call us from India, when she needed help counseling rescued Nepali girls. When girls have just come out of a brothel, they don't believe what people are saying to them. They don't know what is real or what's not. I remembered exactly how that felt.

I loved talking to those girls, convincing them that they could trust Smita, that there was hope for them. If they could see that somebody else, somebody from the same background, had already made it home, they would start thinking that maybe they could too.

Chapter 26

Richa's older sister had been trafficked to India around the same time as her. That girl was rescued in 2013. When the older sister came back to Nepal, we learned that Richa's younger sister had also been trafficked in 2008, around the same time that Richa and I were being rescued.

This kind of situation was common in our district, with sisters, mothers and daughters, aunts, nieces and cousins from one family all being trafficked to India. So we were worried - for good reason - about our sisters back in the villages. We also worried about the condition of our parents and brothers, who were dependent on the money we sent from India. We had good reason to fear that our brothers would be forced to become traffickers. It was hard to completely relax into our new lives when we were so concerned about our families back home.

The staff of Apple believed strongly in reuniting girls with their families, but in the early days, they still didn't know how to do family reunions safely when trafficking was involved. Just after we came home to Nepal, Mamata took a course with the District Court, to get a paralegal certificate. In that training, she met a lawyer who had been working for many years in the anti-trafficking field. She asked him how best to do family reunifications.

"For every one of the girls, reuniting with family was the top priority," said Mamata. "But I had a whole different set of worries. Because many families were involved in trafficking their daughters, I was afraid the parents would demand to get their girls back, only to sell them again. I had seen many times the scenario where one day a girl was reintegrated into her family, the next day she was sold again, and the third day she was already back in an Indian brothel!"

The lawyer told Mamata how to do family reunification the right way. You have to include the government, local charities, and the police. When a lot of people are aware of the situation, that prevents families from demanding their girls back and re-trafficking them. Ideally you don't lose any girls, and families become more sensitized and aware.

"Who can change the mindset of Nuwakot? Not you, and not me," said Mamata. "It needs to be a person who comes from that area, and who used to have the same ideas. That is the only person they will listen to: one of their own. I know the language but that is not enough. The Tamang thinking and culture is unique. Only someone who has grown up there can truly understand the mindset of the people. Ever since I learned about the Tamang girls being rescued in Kolkata, I was hoping and praying for them to be the ones who would bring change to their communities. When it came time for family reunions, I was frankly a bit terrified. I couldn't lose a single one of these fifteen dear sisters. That would be a huge defeat. Instead, I wanted them to multiply, to become many more, to sensitize many villagers. Fifteen girls can change a village".

Rose also felt strongly about the importance of reuniting girls with their birth families. "We never take a child's family away," she said. "I know I am somebody important for them, acting *as* a mother. But they also have a mother and father in some village. We always try to honor that relationship, to reunite them and rebuild those relationships. They have everything to gain and nothing to lose. Our kids have one family from birth and one family from Brazil".

Mamata worked hard to set up a reunion for our group, using the guidelines that the lawyer had given her. It took a full two years, during which we had no contact with our families. She connected with an organization in our area called Red Panda to organize a reunification program.

One night at dinner, Mamata announced the good news, that we would be going a few days later to see our families. We were literally speechless, incredibly excited, and also a little nervous. It had been such a long time since we saw our families. For me it had been seven years, for some girls even longer. *Will my family want to see me?* I wondered. *Would they judge and blame me? Will my mother even be there?* That night, we couldn't sleep at all.

In the morning a van came and took us to the district headquarters in Nuwakot. The drive took five or six hours. As soon as we got close, I began searching madly for my family members on the street, but I didn't see them. When we reached the town, Mamata led us into a large building. A homecoming program was planned with the Chief District Officer of Nuwakot, the police, and all family members who were willing and able to come.

It was a big conference hall, a rented room full of chairs. Already there were many people sitting on the chairs. We sat down on chairs in the back. After a few minutes the program started, and families began to enter the hall. Some parents were afraid, or felt ashamed, so they did not come. Or the mother came but the father did not come. Or neither mother nor father but a little brother came. I looked for my family but I didn't see them. I wondered if anyone would come for me. I got a bad, empty feeling inside. My family had not been there for me and I knew it was possible I would be disappointed by them once again.

There were some presentations and talks but I couldn't understand a word of it. My heart was pounding with the prospect of reunion, and with the fear that I might not get the reunion I was hoping for. I looked all around the room to see if anyone was there for me. In true Nepali style, there were a lot of long speeches. But I heard none of them.

I still couldn't see anyone from my family in the crowd. The announcer started calling our names, and the names of the family members who were there for us. Girls cried out in joy when they saw their families. They fell into each other's arms, weeping. Most of us never thought we would meet again in this lifetime. We had no contact with our families when we were in India. We had no idea how they were, or even who was alive or dead.

When they called my mother's name, I was overcome. She was actually sitting just a few rows ahead of me with my brother, but I had not seen her through the crowd. We all went up on the stage and people put kathas around our necks to bless us. I was crying silently. My mother was weeping loudly. My brother said nothing and showed no emotion.

151

We had some conversation there at the conference room. I was asking so many questions, "How is aunty, uncle, cousins, neighbors?"

My mother told me that my grandfather and one aunt had passed away, so I would not be able to meet them. I felt very sad about this. My mother told me, "I searched for you for years, everywhere. I came to Kathmandu so many times. People told me to go to different places, they sent me to different government offices or charities. I went to every one. But I could not find you".

My mother had gone to Maiti Nepal, a well-known charity, looking for me. She had also gone to lesser-known organizations. She was pouring out all her emotions. "I went here and there, people told me to fill out this form, do this or that".

She had a lot of things in her heart and she was pouring them out. We had good conversations, with a lot of crying. My mother never asked me about my time in India or what happened to me there. She didn't ask me then and she has never asked me since. She just wanted me to know that she never gave up on me. She also talked about the relatives who had died, and about my new little brother, and how my sister Dipti was doing.

After a few hours, we went to a hotel. There were rooms booked for all the families. I stayed one night there and had dinner and lunch the next day with my mom and brother. Again, we didn't sleep. I was falling-down tired, and I kept nodding off while my mom was talking.

The next morning, we had to go back to Kathmandu. My mom was very emotional, saying, "Will I ever see you again? Will you ever come back?"

I promised we would meet again soon. Now we had each other's phone numbers and could talk whenever we wanted. I felt both happy and sad as the van drove away. I felt relieved and joyful to have seen my family after so long, but sad to have to say goodbye to them again. I felt heartsick for the lost years and for what had happened since the last time I saw my family. Mostly I was just grateful to get to know them again, to spend time together, and to hear all the things my mom was desperate to tell me.

Chapter 27

Six months later, I asked Silvio if I could go to my village again and see more of my family members. A lady who was a leader in the Apple boy's home volunteered to accompany me. No one else was very keen to go to my village. They were a little afraid, which was normal, because the people in our village are not normal. The village is full of traffickers. They sometimes attack the police if the police go there. People were afraid the villagers would harm us if we went there. I wasn't offended because sadly, it was all true.

In fact, on another visit to my village for a home study, two Apple staff members had been locked in a hut and held for ransom! Silvio had to pretend he was wiring a large amount of money to get them released. After that incident, no one wanted to go to our area.

The Apple team gave me gifts and money for my family. I bought some pots and clothes and food for my mother. We took a bus this time. Returning to my small village was another milestone for me. I hadn't seen it in six years. The reunion had been in a larger town in the district, because we girls came from many different small villages all over the district. *Would my village be the same? How would people look? How would they treat me?*

When I was in Kolkata, and in Kathmandu, I always used to close my eyes and remember my village. I imagined it all the time, to comfort myself. When I actually saw it, it was quite emotional. It was also quite different.

When I was little, there were no roads to the village. No vehicles could reach there. But things were beginning to change. Now there were roads where there were no roads before. The houses were starting to look a little better.

My mother and my little brother came to meet the bus. This was the first time I met my little brother, who was six years old. We went first to my older brother's house, the old family home where we grew up. Streams of people came to meet me, to see how I was looking.

Since we only had two days, we decided to hike up to my mom's house. It was another hour's walk on steep mountain paths. It was already dark by the time we reached it. My mother had cooked good food for me. I was grateful and it gave the day a mood of celebration. But it also brought up some painful memories, of all the nights - months and years of nights - without proper food to eat, and with no adult in the home to cook for me.

The lady from Apple was freezing cold up in that mountain cottage. There weren't a lot of blankets in our home, so I gave her my blanket and then I was cold. Again, my mom and I spent the whole night talking. My mom kept sharing the same things over and over. She needed to repeat them, like it was a prayer or a petition.

I felt the weight of her regret for what happened to me, for her role in what happened through her neglect and abandonment. I love my mother and she is not a bad person. She had some mental issues, some depression. More than that, she was the product of a society that was broken. The traditional values of our community had been twisted. My mother grew up in that, and then she was widowed as a young woman. I could see that her sorrow and guilt were eating her up inside, and again I made the choice to forgive.

"It's not your fault what happened, Mom," I told her many times that night. By morning, her spirit seemed a little lighter.

By then, I had been living for several years in the healthy and functional family environment of Apple. I was old enough, and recovered enough, to accept the fact that my biological family was never going to be able to love me the way that I wanted and needed. More than that, they had betrayed me, and they were never going to admit it or take responsibility for their failures which led to my deep suffering.

Thankfully, I did have many people in my life - my Apple family, the IJM team, my school friends, and others - who loved and valued me and who were always there for me. I made the conscious decision to accept love however it comes to me. Ever since I was rescued, there have always been loving arms around me. There is no point in yearning for certain people to love you the way you want. Maybe they never can. It's better to love and to appreciate being loved by the people who are actually there for you.

That poor lady from Apple who came with me on that trip! She was an older person, used to the comforts of city life. It was hard for her to walk up and down those mountain trails. I really am thankful to her. Because of her, I got to see my village. Wherever I wanted to go, she went with me. She never complained or asked for a break.

The next morning, we hiked back to my brother's home. I hired a guy from the village to walk beside that lady, propping her up and half-dragging her along those mountain paths. On the last day the four of us went to my maternal grandparents' home. That was really in the middle of nowhere. It took us four hours, up and down more mountain trails. I avoided even looking at the lady from Apple because I was sure she was ready to slap me by the end of the fourth hour of trekking!

My grandparents were so happy to see me. They were crying, holding my hand, saying, "We thought we would never see you again".

We spent one night there and then went back down to my brother's home. I wanted to go see the little school that my father set up. But when I saw it, it was nothing like I remembered. It was in terrible condition. There were just two rooms. One room's door was destroyed and inside the room there was rainwater because the old tin roof was destroyed. Rats and mice had built their own little society.

The trip was all quite emotional but also a relief, because nothing bad happened. No one was held hostage, or anything like that. When it was time to leave, my mother and other relatives were sobbing. I reassured them, "I will come back. Next time I will stay longer".

But it was hard for them to believe. They had grown used to losing me.

I have heard many stories of families not accepting their daughters who have been trafficked. In Sanlaap there were many girls who had been cut off from their families and could never go home. I have heard stories of girls who took their own lives because of that. The only thing you think about when you are in a brothel is being back with your family, and if that is taken from you, it can be too much to bear.

Some people think that trafficked girls are unclean and should not be touched. But in our community, trafficking has become so normalized that families accept girls back easily. For more than twenty-five years, girls from Nuwakot District have been going to India, and eventually they send back money, or bring back money.

I have mixed feelings about this. On the one hand, it is good that families accept girls back, and welcome them with love. On the other hand, it is a twisted situation that forced prostitution is seen as an acceptable career option. It shocks me that the villagers can take trafficking so lightly. It is completely normal for them.

I never expressed anger to anyone in my family in the early days of being reunited with them. I knew that they really didn't understand that trafficking is wrong. They were totally blind to the darkness of it, to the anguish it causes.

But on that second visit, I did say something to my mom about what happened in India. She was criticizing another girl from the village, saying, "That girl, her family says she didn't send any money".

I just had to speak up then. "These village people, they only care about money," I said. "They don't see what we have to do in India. They don't see how harsh our life is there."

My mother really had no idea how hard it was. I told her a small part of what my life was like there, and she tried to understand. I told her about a brothel madam who is from our village. "I am very upset with that lady. She never treated me well. We had to see customers all day and night. We never had enough to eat. We had to spend nights on the roof, a dark and scary place. We weren't allowed to sleep enough. We never went outside. Our bodies were hurt. Our spirits were hurt worse."

But no matter what I said, my mother could only understand a small portion of it. Between her and reality is a screen. Her mind is not right. She believes the village perspective more than mine. That is hard for me. Still to this day, she doesn't seem to truly understand how bad it was. My mother, like others from my village, doesn't have a lot of experience of the world. The villagers have their own way of life, and that is all they know. What happens to us girls in India is outside of their imagination.

Perhaps for my mother to truly comprehend what her own child suffered is just not possible.

I feel there is a dark energy in the village that has covered people's minds. They don't understand that trafficking is wrong. They just believe the things they have heard since ancient times. People say that in ancient times, kings used to take girls from our area into India, as concubines. People take a certain pride in this. But ancient or modern, there is nothing romantic about trafficking and rape. It is a social and spiritual sickness that infected the community and made people blind to the suffering of their sisters and daughters.

I returned to Kathmandu more motivated than ever to bring awareness and change to my people.

Chapter 28

Motivated by my visit to the village and what I saw there, I dedicated myself even more to my studies. I was now in Class 10, and it was extremely challenging. I didn't have the advantage of a solid early education, so I was always playing catch-up.

Sometimes, I also had to struggle against my own dark memories and destructive beliefs. My mind would get cluttered with a crowd of negative thoughts. *How could this have happened? This is all your fault because you are a bad person. You made the choice to run away to India and brought all the problems upon yourself. You are broken and will never be okay. Nobody has ever loved you and no one ever will.*

I would re-enact the violence of the brothel in my mind, over and over (always in the middle of the night), and wake up feeling utterly drained and exhausted, as if I had actually just experienced it. Sometimes I had day nightmares. I saw a lot of naked men when I was in India, and I used to see those images again in my mind. It was re-traumatizing. As I grew older, I learned how to cope with the negative thoughts and the nasty images.

Now, when dark thoughts and images start circling through my mind, I literally shake them out of my head. I move my head quickly from side to side and shake those destructive thoughts and images right out of there. It sounds strange but it works! Or I join in an activity. I get busy with something else, anything else, to distract myself and break the pattern. I change my scenery. I walk outside or simply move to another room in order to interrupt the downward spiral.

Through counseling, I learned that re-living the trauma is a natural reaction to trauma, and I also learned how to control it. I refuse to become my own worst abuser by re-traumatizing myself constantly. I try not to dwell on the mistakes of the past (mine or other people's), but instead to look for ways to save tomorrow.

As hard as it was at times, I kept my eyes on the prize. I needed not just high school but a college degree if I was going to achieve my dream of opening a school in the village. When I finally graduated high school in 2015, at age 20, it was the proudest moment of my life.

For years I had been planning and visualizing and praying about my dream. I talked about it endlessly to anyone who would listen. I am sure my sisters in Home Three were driven a little crazy by my obsession with this subject, but they were too nice to complain. My dream has been a big part of my healing. It has given me a reason to live on this earth and a goal that keeps me from getting stuck in trauma or regrets about the past.

At first. I thought I would be able to work in partnership with the government to open a school in the village. But as I learned about the realities of government school systems in Nepal, I changed my mind. If I worked within the government school system, I wouldn't have the decision-making power. I probably wouldn't be allowed to use the school for community awareness about trafficking, especially given the fact that the traffickers in my village are so powerful and politically connected.

There are so many rules and regulations in the government school system, and there can be a lot of corruption, especially in remote areas. I had this vision of the school being a beacon of light and love in the community. I couldn't imagine the government going for that. So, I made the decision that I would purchase property and build my own school.

My dream evolved into opening a private school which can give a high quality, free or low-cost education up to the secondary level. I want the next generation of my village to get a good education so that their future can be full of hope and opportunity. I want them to have a different concept of life, of themselves, and of money than their parents and grandparents. I want to try my best to educate every girl in my community, so they do not need to go through what I went through. I want to make them capable of earning a good living without being involved in trafficking and prostitution.

The children of my area have to walk two or three hours up and down on slippery paths and over dangerous bridges to get to school. Rainy season is especially dangerous for them. Many children live in areas where construction of a school is not possible due to lack of roads and dangerous paths. For these children, I would need to build a hostel.

My dream is also for adults. I want to offer adult education so that people can learn reading and writing, and other skills with which they can improve their financial situation.

Young and naive as I was, I was confident it would all work out. My only worry was whether I would be able to get enough education to manage a school. Then I learned that raising funds for such a big project was actually the bigger challenge. It would cost over a hundred thousand dollars to buy land and construct a small building. Yikes! I had no money, no connections and no idea how to raise the kind of money I would need.

Chapter 29

Then, out of a terrible crisis, opportunities arose.

In 2015 and 2016, a series of massive earthquakes hit Nepal. The day the first earthquake hit was terrifying. The ground was moving up and down like waves on a beach. There was a noise like a freight train. People were screaming and running out of their houses. You never realize, until you are in a massive earthquake, how much you depend on the ground underneath your feet as a solid, unmoving thing. When you can't count on even that, it is deeply unsettling.

Another major quake came the following week, and many more aftershocks over the next six months. Over nine thousand people died, twenty-five thousand were injured, and 2.8 million were displaced. The Nepalese economy ground to a halt. Tourism, a major source of income for Nepal, still has not recovered.

Two hundred kids and staff from the Apple homes moved into the basketball court and playground of the school. And there we stayed for three weeks. No one wanted to go back inside, and it wasn't safe to do so, until the aftershocks stopped and the buildings could be inspected. Hundreds of people were sharing the school's few bathrooms for several weeks. Young and old were sleeping on the ground. Children were terrified.

There was a wonderful outpouring of support from around the world. One group that came was a group of Brazilians from New Zealand. They came to build earthquake-proof houses for people in need. The Apple family decided to offer this opportunity to four girls from my village. I accompanied the group as a translator, and to help them identify people most in need of help. We worked together in the village for a week, and during that time, I shared my story and my dream with the group. They became very committed to my dream. It became their dream too, and when they went back to New Zealand, they began raising funds to construct the school building.

I asked Silvio if he would help me publish a book about my story. He helped me find Rafael Marques, a Brazilian author who helped me write a book in Portuguese. Rafael came to Nepal just after the earthquake to write the book with me. It got published in Brazil, and then I was invited to Brazil to speak in three states at different churches and events. We made several thousand dollars from book sales. Through the speaking engagements in Brazil, a few incredibly generous people heard my story and felt compelled to give. That was how I raised my first twenty thousand dollars, to use for buying the land for my school.

After the earthquakes, I became worried about my own sister Dipti, back in the village. Dipti was then eleven years old, the most vulnerable age for a girl in our village. I went to the Apple leaders and asked if Dipti could come live at Apple and get an education. They agreed, so I brought her from the village to Kathmandu.

Dipti started her education and was doing well. But suddenly, my mother and stepfather called and asked me to send Dipti back to the village because they needed her to work on the farm. Dipti herself wanted to go back. I talked and pleaded with her until my throat was sore, explaining all the benefits and opportunities that would come her way if she stayed in Kathmandu and got an education.

But Dipti had grown up in the village, with a very different idea of what her life should be like. Her life plan was to work in the fields and marry young. And at age twelve, Dipti got married. There was nothing I could do to stop it. I was too late. The village had gotten to her first. She had absorbed all of the twisted beliefs about what a girl was good for.

My sister's experience made me even more impatient to open my school. The village needed a school where girls like Dipti could learn from early childhood that there were possibilities for their lives other than child marriage or trafficking.

My goal is to buy a parcel of land, and build the school buildings slowly, brick by brick. Though I wish I could do everything this very second, I know that many times in life, we have to wait on God's timing. It's not easy to wait. We feel very urgent about what we want to do. But it is a good thing to be patient and see what time brings us. Also, we should work on what we really want from our innermost heart. Work on what gives you peace and joy. Hard times will surely come, but they will surely also pass with time.

Chapter 30

As I was raising funds for my school in the village, I also started college, majoring in Education. It was even harder than high school, because now many of the readings and exams were in Nepali. Nepali is one of my native languages, but I'm not strong at reading and writing Nepali script.

On the bright side, I felt like I was gaining momentum. I was focused on one thing, and one thing only: my school. And college was going to get me much closer to achieving it.

On my first day of college, I was beside myself with joy and excitement. Unfortunately, things got off to a rough start. The college accountant noticed that my address was a children's home. He asked me why I lived at Apple and not with my family. Because I had been living for a long time in such an open, trusting, and trustworthy community, I made the mistake of telling the accountant the truth about my background. He seemed much too interested in my story, and I realized that I made a mistake by telling him. He made indecent suggestions to me then, and many times after. He called me at all hours, bothering me and making nasty remarks. I learned then that I needed to be a lot more careful about sharing my story.

I knew that I needed training and experience to fulfill my dream, and I wanted to start giving back to those who had done so much for me. So when I was offered a job at the Apple school, I jumped at the chance. At first, I was assigned to be a substitute teacher and to assist with administration. Then, I was appointed as the teacher of the Special Class, the very place where I started my own education at Apple.

My class included a wide range of students. I had eight and nine-year-olds who had just come from the village and didn't speak Nepali, and girls in their late teens who had just returned from India. Both groups were at times sullen, confused, and traumatized. It took every ounce of patience to motivate them, hold their attention and guide them through the difficult first year of school. It was one of the most frustrating and challenging things I had ever done, and also one of the most rewarding.

I had a very specific and detailed plan and timeline for reaching my goal of opening the school. I figured it would take me another two years to move up to the village, and once there, I could finish my college degree online, while getting the school going. I wasn't going to let myself be distracted by boys, or drama with my family, or anything else. I was a woman on a mission.

But then...

Six months after I started college, a friend came to visit from the village. Her mobile phone was broken and she asked me to go with her to the repair shop. There was a guy working there, who recognized me from college. Yogendra was his name. I didn't pay much attention to him. We just had a short conversation about the mobile phone. When we returned the next day to pick it up, Yogendra asked me about my classes, and how I

169

liked college. We had a long conversation with him and his friend. I still didn't realize it, but apparently Yogendra really liked me.

"How come you're not studying for exams? I asked him. "They're coming up soon".

I don't know how I knew this about him, that he wasn't preparing for his exams. Somehow I just sensed it. This really made an impact on Yogendra. It made him feel that I knew him already, like I could read his mind.

"When I saw Anjali's face in the shop, I honestly don't know what happened. I just wanted to talk with her. I just... knew," said Yogendra.

By then, the mobile had been fixed, but Yogendra called and asked us to come back to the shop a third time to make a final adjustment to the phone. In truth, he just wanted to see me again. When he could think of no more reasons to get me into the repair shop, he started trying to run into me at college. After six days of 'chance' meetings, he finally asked me to go on a date with him.

I said, "Thank you but No. I like you as a friend, not as a boyfriend".

I had no intention of getting involved in a relationship that could distract me from my studies and my dream. I wasn't even sure I wanted to date or get married at all. I had such bad experiences with men in the past. I felt that the single life would probably be best for me.

Yogendra was cool about it. He stayed always by my side, as a good friend. After two months, I gave him my Facebook ID, and he started messaging me. By then it was wintertime and still dark in the early morning. I was a little nervous about walking to college alone in the pitch black. Our classes started at 6:00 am but I would arrive late, to avoid walking in the dark. Yogendra noticed and asked why I was always late. He offered to walk with me. He used to wake up at 4:00 am just to do that.

For six months, our friendship grew. Every so often, Yogendra would ask again if I would be his girlfriend. Each time I said "No, I love you as a friend".

For more than a year he kept trying. We had a lot of conversations through letters. That felt safer. Yogendra really was a good friend to me. I told him about the college accountant who had been harassing me after I told him about my background. Yogendra went and talked with him. I don't know exactly what was said, but the accountant never called me again after that.

I rejected Yogendra as a boyfriend for two reasons. First, it was a little hard to believe that he was sincere. I had been focused on my studies and on my life in Home Three, which was an all-girl environment. I didn't have that much familiarity with the outside world. It was hard for me to trust people, due to lots of betrayals in the past. Secondly, Yogendra didn't have the relationship with God that I had, and I really wanted to marry a guy who shared that.

Also, my family in the village was being small-minded about it, because Yogendra was from a different caste. People in our village only marry other Tamangs. My mother would always say, "It's not good, it won't work out. What will people say?"

About a year after we met, on Yogendra's birthday, I finally agreed to go out with him for tea. We went to a hotel near the college and afterwards I agreed to visit his home. I met his father and stepmother. And from that day on, I started loving him back. After a few more weeks, he asked again if I would go out with him. I said "I already accepted you, silly! Why do you think I went to your house?"

I changed my mind about dating Yogendra because I saw his faithfulness. His love never wavered. Yogendra was always beside me that first year. He never pressured me. He was just right there, in case I ever needed him. I'm a curvy type, and some guys don't go for that. Yogendra loved me just the way I was. I shared honestly with him about my background, about everything that happened in India. We were both aware that some people would talk badly about me, and about him for being with me. He couldn't care less what people would think or say.

I also told Yogendra that if he wanted to be with me, he would have to go to this remote and lawless village and work with me there for years. Very few people would wish to do that. I told him that I wanted to be with a Christian guy who was committed to growing in his faith. He was okay with all of it. He didn't care what people would think, what happened in the past, or what crazy adventures I had planned for our future. He was willing to stand with me through all of it.

In December Yogendra went to Qatar to work and earn some money. A few months after he left, I traveled to my village to retrieve some records from the old school that my father started. A lady came to my mom's

172

house from a nearby village. She started to talk to me about her son. She wanted me for him, as his bride. "You can marry my son now, and then you can go to Kathmandu and finish your studies, and later come back here," she said.

It was like she was offering me an advance on the marriage: Pay now, pick up later! Her son was just a teenager, eight or nine years younger than me. I told her very directly, "I am not ready to get married, and I am not interested in your son. I just came to get some papers".

But she wouldn't take no for an answer, and she would not leave. She came at 8:00 pm and stayed until midnight, talking nonstop the whole time. Tamangs are very persistent. The annoying lady had brought some wine to my mom. "Please take your wine and go," I told her.

She finally left, but she said she would return the next day. "Please don't bother!" I said, "I am not going to marry your son".

When at last she left, I was really worried, because once again my family were not standing up for me. It is common in our area for girls to be kidnapped and forced to marry. That was what I was always hiding from when I was little. I had no confidence that my mom and stepfather would intervene if that lady tried to abduct me and force the marriage.

It made me feel angry, and also terribly alone. No one was standing with me. In normal life, when you say 'No', people understand and back off. But in the village, you can say 'No' a hundred times and still people will keep trying to convince you.

At 1:00 in the morning, I called Mamata and woke her up, because I was feeling so upset that the situation seemed to be escalating, and my family was not standing by me. Also, I wanted her to know what was going on, so she would know where to look if I suddenly went missing. "Stay strong, sister. They will do nothing," she reassured me.

After I finished the call, there were still ten or twelve people outside my mother's house. Every few minutes they would knock on the door with some new excuse. They were hoping to wear me down. My mother, as usual, was not able to protect me at all. She was not making them leave. She was afraid of making enemies by refusing them.

Eventually, I lost my temper with her. "Please stop this ridiculous behavior! You cannot tell me who to marry or make me go with these people. If you don't want to stand up for me, then fine. I am going to open this door, but I am not going with these people. I am going to make them leave".

There was quite a large group of people there, with their food and wine, settling down for a long winter's night. They got excited when I opened the door. "Come on, let's go," they shouted.

I told them I had no intention of going with them. One lady, a relative of mine, started to force gold earrings and jewelry on me. She grabbed me and tried to put the earrings on me, because in our culture, if you put gold jewelry on a woman, then it seals the deal. When that failed, she tried to sneak money and gold jewelry under my pillow. I was crying with frustration and anger. I called my brother on the phone and begged him to come and help. "If it continues, call me back," he said.

But he didn't come over. I felt like I had no one. It brought up all the hurt from before. The nonsense continued long into the night. The villagers kept talking, trying to convince me. They were relentless. I was beside myself. I stayed inside, afraid of all the people in the yard. Finally, I couldn't take it anymore. I came out and started talking very loudly and clearly. "Please go away and do not come back. My decision is final. I am not going to marry this guy".

Everything that happened in India was coming back, circling around and around in my head. I was fearful of being taken again. It was hard to breathe, but I hid it and kept my voice strong and clear. A few hours later, at 5:00 am, I left to go back to Kathmandu, feeling broken and very alone.

As soon as I got home, I called Yogendra. He was very supportive and gradually helped me to calm down. He had proposed marriage several times before that, but I wasn't ready to say yes. I realized then that he was the one I could turn to in a crisis. He was the one I chose to call to make me feel better. His love for me was pure. He saw beauty in me that I couldn't see in myself. He recognized me. I knew then that he was the one for me, and I accepted his proposal.

Chapter 31

Our engagement was pretty short. We got married a few months later in June of 2017. I was a little surprised when not everyone supported the idea at first. Many of my friends and mentors at Apple were thrilled for me, that I had found someone to share my life, a man who didn't have any concerns or judgments about my background. Others were worried that I was too young to be getting married, and that I needed more time to develop myself, and finish my education. Everybody seemed to have a different opinion and I became extremely flustered, doubting myself and my decision. I really did not know what to do. I hated that I couldn't make everyone happy.

Finally, Silvio sat me down and gave me some good advice. "You will never be able to please everyone, so please God, and please yourself," he said. "If you live according to your own values, and your own sense of God's will for your life, it doesn't matter what anyone else thinks".

Yogendra's family was also none too happy about our engagement. They liked me as a person, but weren't comfortable with me being a Christian, and coming from such a strange and unfamiliar tribal background. Thankfully, they didn't say too much about it.

My family, on the other hand, made a huge fuss. They weren't ready to accept Yogendra because he was from another caste. He was not Tamang. "What will people say?" they asked me, again and again.

I explained to them very frankly, that when girls are in a brothel, they have to spend their life, their blood, a lot of nights, with every kind of man. It doesn't matter if the man is sick or healthy, dark or light, young or old, thin or fat, ugly or handsome, clean or dirty. It doesn't matter what caste he is from. You just have to go with him.

"Nobody said anything about caste then because these guys were paying money," I said. "You were not angry at that time. You don't say it's wrong' when your daughters and sisters are spending nights with all those men. But now when I want to marry a guy who loves me, who is from another caste, you are making a thing of it. That is totally crazy!"

After I said that, they kept quiet.

I brought Yogendra to the village to meet my family. We had a nice visit. Everyone was polite. I can't say that they embraced him wholeheartedly, but they seemed to have gotten used to the idea. If they had a complaint, they kept it to themselves. I think people in my family are a little afraid of me, now that they know I am not afraid to speak the truth. The truth is a shield and a sword, as Smita once told me.

At the wedding, no one said anything negative at all. It was a beautiful and perfect day.

There were some people there from my village, members of my extended family, including some who are probably still involved in trafficking. So the wedding had sharp contrasts: traffickers and survivors, anti-trafficking activists, rich and poor, Nepalis and Brazilians and Americans and other nationalities too.

There were four hundred people there, all the kids and staff from Apple homes, past and present. My birth family, and my spiritual family were there to celebrate with me. Silvio and Rose walked me down the aisle, but everything was delayed by at least an hour because I could not stop crying and kept messing up my makeup.

Nepalis go in for long wedding ceremonies, and this was no exception. The service was three hours long. A few times I became overcome with emotion, or nervous, but then I just looked out over the crowd full of my sisters and brothers, and I felt their love coming over me in waves. My heart was as full as it has ever been.

Before the wedding, and during the first few months of our marriage, being in an intimate relationship brought up a lot of trauma for me. For people who have been trafficked, it is hard to believe that sexual relations can be good or safe. It took a lot of counseling, and talking it through with Yogendra, and hearing over and over that physical intimacy can be good when it is done lovingly and properly, for me to feel comfortable. I became able to face the same situation, but in a positive way. I found a way to write a new story with the same words.

One year after our wedding, something just incredible happened. I was pretty sure I wouldn't be able to get pregnant, because of the damage to my body from the brothel time. Yogendra knew this, and he accepted the possibility that I wouldn't be able to conceive. He didn't mind. We planned to adopt if I wasn't able to get pregnant.

I'm not the most organized about remembering the dates of my period, and because of that, it took me a few months to realize that my period had stopped. I took a pregnancy test, and to my great surprise it was positive. But still I couldn't believe it. We went to a clinic and they confirmed it. I was two months pregnant.

We were overjoyed, but quietly so. We knew that carrying a baby to term still might not be possible for me. For six or seven months, I managed my expectations. I told myself that maybe I was just gaining some weight, and not to get too excited.

Life is never easy, and you shouldn't expect it to be. So of course, my baby came by C-section in the middle of the COVID outbreak. Because of the virus, no one from the Apple family or my village family or Yogendra's family could come and see us. It was just me and Yogendra in the hospital alone, and then the three of us back home alone. That was a little disappointing, but it didn't matter so much. We had each other, and this beautiful, healthy baby boy. Of all the miracles I had experienced in my life, nothing compared to this one.

The first time I saw my son's face, tears streamed down my cheeks. Those tears contained so many things - the broken dreams of a lonely, hungry village child, the despair of a trafficked twelve-year old, the sudden flash of hope of a rescued girl, the healing power of faith, of a family found just in time, the surprising love of a good man, the miracle of new life and the promise of a bright future, for all of us, together. I had no words. I still have no words. My child is a shining light in my life that I never could have imagined. He was not in my dreams in my darkest hours, but surely the possibility of him was one of the things that kept me alive.

Chapter 32

Everybody is born on the earth with his or her own rights. The person who steals, kills, or sells girls for money - to enjoy a good life at the cost of destroying others' lives - has a heart of stone.

Everyone is not born with equal knowledge, character, and ability but every human being should have equal rights. Everyone should have opportunities.

In my childhood, I was never allowed to speak up. I was always kept in fear of others. From age seven to thirteen, I lived without getting a hug, love, proper food, education or basic care and protection. I lived those six years in constant fear. I was never told that I have rights - to live freely and to get an education.

I can't even explain how much I was scared of others in my childhood. I was taught to fear the police. I was told that if the police found me, they would take and beat me for no reason. At age eleven, I lived every minute scared of the boys from the other village, who came every day to take me by force into a child marriage. I spent a year hiding in the jungle. My life became so miserable with that constant fear that I became ready to go with the traffickers. I was ready to do anything to relieve the fear. I escaped from that situation, only to find myself in a much worse one.

My life again was filled with fear, of the brothel managers, of the clients who were free to do whatever they wanted to me, and of the police, who were only too willing to take their share. I was told not to trust anyone claiming to want to help me. I was convinced that they would kill me or lock me away, and I would never see my home or mother again.

Today I am so much stronger. It still scares me to share my views openly as I still long for people's love, affection and support. It may take a lifetime for all parts of myself to be healed.
But I am now ready to fight with all my energy and love.

The light of education will bring a new way of life to my people. If equal opportunities are provided to both boys and girls, they will be able to contribute equally to their family and the country. I pray that my dream can change even one person's life. What I want for my community is not just small changes but a complete transformation, from a brutal and unjust system to a healthy and whole society, in which everyone's well-being is equally important.

The brokenness of our community is not any one person's fault. It is a result of the weakness of education and lack of awareness. Whatever happened in the past can't be undone, but we can save the upcoming generation. We can change tomorrow, and in order to save the next generation of girls, we must change the concepts and minds of the entire community - men and women, boys and girls.

Today I have a beautiful life. Even before I knew God, He was watching over me and my life. I was saved from the brothel because He sent people to rescue me, counsel me, get me back to Nepal, educate me, and build a home for me, with a new family to nurture me back to life.

I have learned to love, laugh, sing, and speak my mind freely. I have healed in such a way that I am able to forgive the people who sold me, betrayed me, and took advantage of my innocence. I forgive the uncle who abused me by touching my body parts, and the one who tried to keep a sexual relationship by giving me things and pretending we were close. I forgive the people who always said good things about India which were untrue. I forgive my parents who didn't take good care of me. I forgive the boys who tried to force me into marriage at the age of eleven.

I forgive the men who took me in India and sold me for a few hundred dollars, and the women who bought me for the brothel. I forgive the people who saw me hidden under a bed but closed their eyes and the people who kept me for ten months, pretending to educate me, only to send me on to a brothel the day my period started. I forgive the woman who took me into the brothel and made me do the work, the managers who controlled the brothel, the Nepali men who came as customers but had no compassion for their sisters enslaved there. I forgive all the customers who fulfilled their desires, using the body and soul of a child, and all the people who were walking close beside me and using me with their eyes closed.

I forgive them all, not for their sake, but for mine. It is the only way I can be free

Today, I can go anywhere freely without fear because I am educated. I know my rights, and I have a strong identity. Since my own life has been so completely changed, I believe that change is possible, even in situations that seem hopeless and stuck. Every day that I am given in life, my aim will be to make positive changes, in girls' lives, in my community, in the society as a whole.

You have to first give your all, and then you can say whether something is possible or impossible. It depends on us, how we take a situation. Even in a hard time, if we think, this is a normal and manageable thing, then we can indeed solve it. But if we get overwhelmed and see it as a major problem, then we won't be able to overcome it. It depends on us whether we choose long-term joy or two days of happiness. If we think something is possible and work hard, then maybe some change will come. If we do nothing, then definitely nothing will change.

The changes I wish to see in my village are large, and the system of trafficking is deeply rooted. Change may not come quickly but I believe if I work hard with all my energy and love, then after many years change will come. Future generations of girls will live in peace.

The terrible things that happened to me, happened. They were out of my control, and they cannot be undone. I choose to release the power of these events to hurt me, by focusing on the things I can control: my dream, my attitude, my values, my faith, and my commitment to the next generation.

No one spoke up when I was trafficked to India. No one stood in the way to prevent it. But then, *many* people stood in the way, blocking the path to destruction.

Don and Vic spent months and years putting a system in place to rescue girls from brothels. Smita, the operatives, and many others risked their lives to rescue us. Indrani created the Sanlaap shelter where we were able to begin our healing journey. Rupa, Swapnil, Trishna and the other counselors spent countless hours, and used all their imagination to pull us out of our despair and to help us find hope again. Mamata fought for us in courtrooms and offices from Nuwakot to Kolkata and brought me back home to Nepal. Silvio and Rose spent their lives building a home where I could heal, and gathering a big, loving family to wrap me in love. Yogendra stepped up to walk beside me, as a best friend, husband and valiant protector, filling my life with more love, and making it possible for pure joy to come in the form of our son.

And now I will stand in the way, for all the little girls of my village, so that their lives can be hopeful and full of opportunity. May they never know such darkness and hopelessness as I have seen.

Having such a destination to reach gives me a reason to live. And that is my justice.

Today

The Dream

In the summer of 2020, I purchased land for my school, and we broke ground on the first school building in December. I moved back up to the village in early January 2021. We are continuing to raise funds to construct the school buildings and boarding hostel, and to operate the school. It will be called the Hasta Memorial School, in honor of my father whose name was Hasta.

Please help save the next generation of girls by donating to our campaign on GoFundMe.

www.gofundme.com/f/spring-school

Don Gerred

Don returned to America in 2009, as living in Kolkata was taking a toll on his family. After six years in Cincinnati, the Gerreds felt called to return to South Asia in 2015. They lived for three years in Kathmandu, near the Apple of God's Eyes family. Don worked for the Nepal office of Justice Ventures International, which continues investigations and raids of brothels in India. Don's daughter Grace played the viola at my wedding. It was beautiful! Don and his family are now back in Cincinnati, where Don works at Crossroads Church, a faith community that is passionate for social justice.

"We need to keep the pressure on - for rescuing girls and prosecuting traffickers," says Don. "A brothel is a business. Specifically, it is a retail space, and the owners are going to fill that space with the most valuable 'product' possible, and that is young girls. As long as brothels are allowed to operate with impunity, the demand for the most valuable commodity - children - will also exist. These children are counting on us, and we can't stop searching until all of them are found".

Smita Singh

After seeing many survivors placed in government shelters where their needs were not met, Smita was compelled to create a different kind of home in Kolkata. In 2009 she set up Mahima home and two years later, she left IJM to run it full time. "All the things that I thought did not work, I did the opposite," said Smita.

From that one home, Smita went on to build three more, as well as a drop-in center in Sonagachi. Mahima Homes now provides shelter, counseling, and other services to over two hundred girls and boys. Tragically, our beloved Smita passed away from COVID-19 in July of 2020. We dedicate this book to her.

Indrani Sinha:

Indrani Sinha, founder of Sanlaap, passed away in 2015. Many strong women that she mentored, inspired, rescued and nurtured through Sanlaap carry on her beautiful work even after her death.

Rupa Chetri:

After counseling the Tamang girls at Sanlaap, Rupa decided to move back to Nepal with her husband and children, so that she could remain close to the Nepali girls she had counseled in Kolkata and continue to be part of our family. She and her husband hosted Friday night dinners for all of the girls from our rescue for many years. Rupa realized that she needed to study and learn the system in order to work within it, so she pursued a master's degree in Clinical Psychology.

"I still remember the smiles on the girls' faces when they waited for me every Thursday at Sanlaap," Rupa says. "They were transformed by the work we did together, but I was equally transformed. When I heard their stories and saw how loyal they still were to their family members, that made me see this as a ministry, not just as a job. It is very easy for survivors to give up on their dreams, because of the trauma and all the challenges they face as they heal: going back to school at a late age, PTSD, ongoing disappointments and rejections from their family and community, and so on. So my role has been to be the 'dreamkeeper', to record their dreams and then continuously encourage them, to remind them who they are".

Mamata Tamang:
Mamata served three terms as the Chairperson of Nepalese Home, the Nepali arm of The Apple of God's Eyes. Currently she is acting as an Advisor to Nepalese Home and as the principal of the Apple School. She continues to provide all the love and support she can to the hundreds of children in Apple Homes. She is the mother of eleven-year- old Mayalu and raising her niece and nephew.

"I am so proud of all my girls. They are brilliant," Mamata says. "The biggest challenge of my work is getting girls to pursue their education so they can be independent. They get frustrated and we are not able to change their mindset that they are getting older and need to work and earn money to help their families, or that they have to get married because everyone else is already married. To keep them focused is my biggest challenge. The most joyful part of my work is the relationships. Most of the girls who grew up with me are achieving something in their lives, and that makes all the hard work worthwhile".

Silvio and Rose Silva:

Silvio and Rose are still living and working in Kathmandu. They have worked hard to cultivate leaders for the organization from within Nepal, so that The Apple of God's Eyes can be sustainable in the long term. Their greatest joy is to see the kids that they have raised becoming doctors and nurses, accountants and businesspeople, teachers, social workers, mothers and fathers, designers and tailors, bakers and engineers. Most of all they love to see their kids stand up and speak up for each other, and to protect the next generation of Nepali children.

The Traffickers and Case

Three people in India were successfully prosecuted in our case. One has since been released and two are still serving sentences for the trafficking of minor children. After I and the other Tamang the girls went home to Nepal, the court case went on for another eight years. For a long time, the brothel owner couldn't be found. He got bail, he kept absconding, so that delayed the case a lot. It's a very corrupt courthouse. But finally, with the testimonies we gave when we were living in India, and the testimonies we traveled back to Kolkata to give, three people were convicted. The brothel owner and two of the managers were each sentenced to seven to ten years.

Trafficking in India

There are still huge numbers of young girls being trafficked into India, particularly in private homes and small brothels. Now unfortunately there is likely to be a huge spike because of the COVID-19 virus, Nepal's earthquakes, Bengal's cyclone and struggling economies throughout South Asia. More Nepali girls are now being sent to Delhi, Mumbai, and to smaller cities and towns. Many are trafficked as domestic workers. A recent research project revealed that over 40% of pimps in India say they are able to source minor girls for customers.

The Tamang Girls

Richa has graduated from Class 12, and is doing vocational training.

Jesika is doing vocational training in tailoring and baking. She plans to return to the village to help me with the school.

Tanu is in college and planning to be a lawyer. She hopes to advocate for Nepali survivors in India.

Ruksa is working in the Apple tailoring unit.

Bindu is also working in the Apple tailoring unit and raising her son who is now in grade 6.

Sheetal is married, back in the village and living a happy life. She looks forward to helping me with the community outreach projects.

Pemba is the mother of two children and also living in the village happily.

Grishma is the mother of a five-year-old son and living in the village happily.

Rita is also a mother of a child and living in the village happily.

Tiku is happy in the village with two children.

There will be many sisters to welcome me when I move back to the village!

Epilogue

By Co-Author Sarah Symons

I first met Anjali in January 2009, just a few months after she was rescued. My nonprofit, Her Future Coalition, (www.HerFutureCoalition.org) was leading two weeks of therapeutic arts workshops at Sanlaap that winter. We were going to paint a mural, and make puppets, among other projects. As soon as she heard our plan, Indrani decided that out of all the girls at Sanlaap (about 150), she wanted us to work with the Tamang girls. I will forever be thankful to her for making that decision.

The two weeks working with Anjali and the other Tamang girls at Sanlaap shelter were profound for me. I had worked with survivors for several years already, but I had never before encountered such gentle, loving souls. At first when we approached them, they were sitting in a tight circle, set apart from the other girls at the shelter. As we cautiously drew closer, they tightened their ranks. I could see that trust would not be so easily won.

That day, the cook of one of our Indian staff had come to volunteer with us. Her name was Rangita and she was Tamang. None of us knew that we would be working with Tamang girls that day. It was miraculous that we had a Tamang speaker with us. When Rangita began to speak to the girls in their native language, their circle opened, and their eyes lit up. It was the first time they had heard an adult speaking their language with kindness in many years.

Rangita persuaded the girls to come and work on the mural with me and my team. For the next two weeks, we worked together on the mural, and engaged in other therapeutic art projects and educational workshops. Anjali was always right by my side, ready to help with whatever I needed. She was joyful and quick, and so full of love. When it was time for us to leave, she gave me a card she had made, decorated with leaves from the trees in the shelter grounds. It was a picture of a lion. Inside the card, she wrote about her father, his school, and her dream.

That was the last time Her Future Coalition ran workshops at Sanlaap. We started other programs, building a shelter and vocational training centers, and opening Resource Centers for children growing up in red light areas. We began sponsoring the education of survivors and high-risk girls in India and Nepal. Because we were no longer working at the Sanlaap shelter, I never found out what happened to Anjali and the other Tamang girls. It was a great sadness for me.

A few years later, friends from a partner organization in Nepal were visiting our home at Thanksgiving. They were scrolling through photos on an IPAD, briefly describing what or who was in each picture. "That's Eliza, that's Asha, that's her older brother, that's Anjali..."

"Wait!" I shouted. "Is that Anjali Tamang?"

And it was my Anjali! She had been repatriated back to Nepal to the very organization that I partnered with there - Apple of God's Eyes! I ran and found the card that Anjali had made for me on my last day at Sanlaap, with her story written inside. Silvio and Rose confirmed that this was indeed the very same girl.

We arranged a video call and sent some emails back and forth. Then a few months later, when I came to Nepal, Anjali was there to meet me at the Kathmandu airport. She wrapped a katha scarf around my neck, we hugged for at least five minutes, and we've been going through life together ever since.

When Anjali and Silvio asked me to help write a book about her life in English, I jumped at the chance. I have learned so much about love and healing, writing this book with her, and together interviewing all the courageous people who pulled her out of slavery and helped her to heal and to build a beautiful life. I feel blessed to support her college education, to help with the new school, and to call her my daughter.

I can't wait for the next chapter of this incredible life story, as Anjali opens the school in her village in April 2021.

Please walk this journey with us by donating to the school.
www.gofundme.com/f/spring-school

100% of book sales proceeds are also being donated to the school.

Contact us to have Anjali or Sarah speak at your event:
info@HerFutureCoalition.org

Acknowledgments:

Anjali Tamang:

My gratitude firstly goes to Jesus who is my spiritual Father and healing God whose words are hope and strength for my life.

I would like to express my enormous gratitude to my courageous Silvio Uncle, Rose Aunty and Mamata sister whose contributions to my life can't be explained in my little words. They are the people of God whose love changed my life. Once a sister asked me about Apple of God's Eyes, what it meant to me. For a few seconds, I couldn't speak a word and no sound came out of my mouth. I had so much I wanted to say a lot but I didn't know which words could fully express my thankfulness to them. I said "For me, Apple of God's Eyes is a place full of courageous people. Each member from small to big tells me 'May God bless you and your dream and don't let go of your dream'".

I am grateful to my husband Yogendra ('Binod') for his love, friendship and support. He has been a great blessing in my life. He is always there supporting me with his own God-given vision. He loves and respects me and my opinions.

I would like to thank the IJM team: Don, Smita, Rupa, Swapnil, Trishna, Vic, Tapan and many others. God used these brave, selfless people to take me out of that harsh and miserable life. I am here today because they risked their lives and fought with many people to get justice for me and to bring me home to Nepal.

I am grateful to Dr José, my beloved grandfather. He is the one to whom God gave the vision to start Apple of God's Eyes, where I lived for seven years and where I was able to build my future and to heal. I am blessed to know him and to be called his granddaughter.

I am thankful to my respected teachers in Apple of God's Eyes Academy, and also for my earlier teachers at Sanlaap. You have given me the light of education. You have passed on to me the power that it carries.

A special gratitude to my sponsor, co-author, a God- gifted mother, guide, and supporter Sarah Symons. She is someone who is very special for me, a source of courage and positive thoughts for every situation and a person on whose arm I can cry and pour all my emotions without worrying about judgment, who has blessed me in every step of my life. Her hug gives me healing for the rest of the time that I have to spend struggling with different situations in life. She is the one who is writing this book together with me, who decided to bless me and be with me all the ways of my life.

I am grateful to Sanlaap. Sanlaap was my first safe haven, and the people there will always be my family. The aunties, uncles, brothers and sisters there loved me. I am grateful for the lives of Indrani, Tapoti, Chanda, Dadu, and many more.

I am deeply thankful to Mamata, Marcia and Shova Sister who were my home mothers for 7 years at Apple. They were always there for me.

My gratitude to MCM, Dr. Jose's organization in Brazil for blessing me by publishing my story in Portuguese to support my dream. They invested when I didn't have anything and they gave all the money that came from selling the book towards my dream. Special thanks to Rafael Brother for writing my story in Portuguese.

I would like to express my gratitude from the heart to Pastor Joao, his wife Tania and his team from New Zealand. They blessed me by taking my dream as their own, and raising funds through different activities like cooking and selling food, sharing messages with their networks and risking their lives on a challenging, multi-week bicycle ride across New Zealand.

I am grateful to all the brothers, sisters, uncles, and aunties of the Apple of God's Eyes family, in Nepal, Brazil, USA, and around the world. I am thankful to God for this beautiful big family. for choosing me among the millions of people in the world to get this family's love, support and protection.

Sarah Symons:

I too would like to sincerely thank the people listed above, and all the others who helped Anjali and the other Tamang girls to be freed and healed. I especially wish to thank Silvio and Rose, for their tireless efforts on behalf of trafficked and vulnerable girls, for our long partnership and friendship, and for suggesting me as co-author of this book.

I thank my husband John Berger, co-founder of Her Future Coalition, for his constant support and encouragement, while I was working on this book, and always.

Huge gratitude to Heather Deyo, our first reader and editor, for her extremely helpful insights on the book, and on everything in my life. Thanks also to Developmental Editor Jennifer Blanchard.

I am grateful to the Her Future Coalition staff, past and present, for walking with me through all the ups and downs of this long and surprising journey. Thank you, (in chronological order) Alicia, Becky, Tia, Paul, Dianna, Nancy, Soma, Nafiza, Doel, Robin, Maura, Felicity, Sarah, Aslyn, Heather, Sonali, Amanda, Caroline, Toby and Kulsum. Thank you to our dear volunteers and Board members, and special thanks to the incomparable Diane Beale, Crystal Freed and Beth Tiger. Thank you to all our donors and supportive friends who have made the work possible, and made it possible for me to co-write this book.

Lastly, I would like to express my huge gratitude and love for my co-author Anjali Tamang. You inspire me and bring me happiness every day. I always dreamed of having a third child, and when I met you again in Kathmandu, I saw that my dream had come true.

If you enjoyed reading this book, please write a review on Amazon.

It will help us share this story with more people. Thank you!

Made in the USA
Middletown, DE
14 September 2021

48247138R00123